Around America

ALSO BY WALTER CRONKITE

A Reporter's Life

Westwind

Remembering the Moon

Save the Birds
(*With Roger Tory Peterson*)

North by Northeast

South by Southeast

Eye on the World

Around America

A Tour of Our Magnificent Coastline

Walter Cronkite

Drawings by David Canright

W. W. Norton & Company

NEW YORK | LONDON

Printed in the United States of America
FIRST EDITION

For information about permission to reproduce
selections from this book, write to
Permissions, W. W. Norton & Company, Inc.
500 Fifth Avenue, New York, NY 10110.

The text of this book is composed in Berthold Bodoni Old Face
The headlines of this book are composed in Adobe Linotype Didot Headline
Manufacturing by Quebecor Fairfield
Book design by John Bernstein

Library of Congress Cataloging-in-Publication Data

Cronkite, Walter.
Around America: a tour of our magnificent coastline / Walter Cronkite.

p.   cm.

ISBN: 0-393-04083-6

1. United States—Description and travel. 2. Atlantic Coast (U.S.)—Description and travel.
3. Pacific Coast (U.S.)—Description and travel. 4. Gulf Coast (U.S.)—Description and travel.
5. Cronkite, Walter—Journeys—United States. 6. United States—History, Local—Anecdotes.
7. Gulf Coast (U.S.)—History—Anecdotes. I. Title.

E169.04.C74 2001   973'.0946—dc21   00-069563

W. W. Norton & Company, Inc.
500 Fifth Avenue, New York, N.Y. 10110
www.wwnorton.com

W. W. Norton & Company Ltd.
Castle House, 75/76 Wells Street, London W1T 3QT

1 2 3 4 5 6 7 8 9 0

Contents

FOREWORD

7

The Northeast

11

The Southeast

81

The Gulf Coast

129

The West Coast

145

Foreword

THERE ARE NEARLY five thousand miles of it. Almost half of us Americans, 112 million of us, live well within a half-day's drive of it. A large part of our commerce and prosperity depends upon it. Much of our history belongs to it. Almost all those who came to settle this country of ours landed upon it.

It is our coastline, that part of the lower forty-eight states that meets the Atlantic from the giant tides of Passamaquoddy, Maine, to the spectacular sunset of Key West, Florida; that meets the Gulf of Mexico from Key West to Port Isabel, Texas; that meets the Pacific from the wild and rainy bluffs of Cape Flattery, Washington, to sun-drenched San Diego, California.

It may have something to do with the certainty of the evolutionists that the sea was once our home, that we once were amphibians crawling up its shores. At any rate, there seem to be few humans who are not fascinated by it. We are attracted to that boundary where land meets sea — whether from its beaches we watch with near hypnotic fascination as the waves curl ashore or gaze from bluffs above with wonder as, with the fury of the Gods, the waves dash against the rocks below and roar their defiance as they fall back and organize for another try.

Much of our coastline, of course, marks the edge of a vast playground for that portion of us who love boats — a portion that seems to grow larger every year. The boating industry estimates that there are now 6,300,000 boats in our coastal states, and it places their total value at just about three billion dollars. They vary mightily in their cost — from the few hundred dollars of a rowboat (or even less when home-built) to the multimillion dollar pleasure palaces, some of which even boast fireplaces. They also vary widely in their purposes, and it is a maxim that the pleasure they render their owners bears no relation whatsoever to their cost.

In the quiet waters behind harbor breakwaters, children barely out of rompers sail with frowning intensity in their eight-foot training boats as the bigger boats and older skippers, surely with no greater satisfaction, steer around them on their way out to deeper waters.

There may be no prettier sight than a fleet of sailing boats with their multicolored spinnakers set as they race around the buoys in the outer harbors or the open oceans off our coasts.

Some find a form of modern beauty in the wake of a high-powered speedboat bouncing from wave top to wave top, although this is anathema to most of those who prefer the challenge of olden times exemplified in those vessels propelled solely by the wind. For the sails that propel them, they are called "rag sailors," and it is a

name they relish. They in turn call those powerboats with their engine exhausts "stink pots" — a title not relished among the stink potters.

One of the great mysteries, unsolved as far as I know, is the answer to that question of when a boat is a yacht. The best answer that has crossed my ken is the one delivered to me by a salty yacht salesman on the Annapolis harbor.

"If a man thinks his boat is a yacht, it's a yacht," said he.

In fact, when the assault on our language, spawned by television and the feminist movement, swept down upon us in the latter part of the twentieth century, one of the early words that got caught up in socioeconomic correctness was "yachtsman." It was a word that always had a nice ring to it, conjuring up the picture of a handsome gentleman of uncertain age in proper yachting attire — a billed cap with white top, a blazer and white trousers — the sort of attire seen today only at formal occasions at the ritzier yacht clubs.

But "yachtsman" lost out partly because in the years following

World War II the development of plastics made possible the mass production of boats vastly cheaper than those grand wooden vessels that all were basically one of a kind. "Yachtsman" seemed a little grand in describing the masses that now were able to realize their lifelong dreams of boat ownership.

And on the heels of that came the feminist movement's program to avoid male-specific words like "yachtsman" to describe those of the opposite gender. So boating magazine writers in a desperate effort to avoid the awkward "yachtswoman" came to "boaters." It seems we are stuck with that word, which is eminently correct, if devoid of elegance.

This volume is about the cruises of one boater who likes to think of himself as a yachtsman, namely me, who has sailed the length of our Atlantic coast, much of our Pacific coast, and, abashedly, only portions of our Gulf coast. What might appear to be short shrift for the Gulf has been solely a matter of geographical convenience, and one of life's great misfortunes is that there is not enough time to sail to everywhere one would desire — and still make a living, that is.

Each of our coasts is unique unto itself: the Atlantic side serrated with its great bays and sounds from the many islands of rock-ribbed Maine to the sandy stepping-stones of the Florida Keys; the Gulf of Mexico coast where the great rivers and meandering streams that drain much of the nation finally find their way through the gentle plains and marshes and bayous to the sea; and the Pacific coast with its almost unbroken wall of spectacular cliffs that reach from its northern tip until finally giving way to the beaches of southern California.

The Northeast

A LL SAILS ARE SET, and they are pulling nicely the big genoa, the staysail, the main, and the little mizzen balancing it all.

It has been like this all night long, a spanking southwesterly of fifteen knots off the port quarter, enough to give us a good turn of speed but not enough to give the Atlantic waves any real punch in their eight-mile fetch from the New Jersey coast. They impart just a little corkscrew effect to keep the helmsman awake in this dogwatch hour right before dawn.

This has been one of the rare perfect passages along the Jersey coast, where any wind from the Eastern Hemisphere can make the Atlantic mighty unpleasant and render the few inlets dangerous of entry.

On this night I'm sure that fresh in my crew's memory is one of my command decisions a few months before on our fall southbound passage. I decided then to seek shelter from an approaching hurricane by running the inlet at Atlantic City.

It was an arguable decision, as my crew's lively discussion proved. But I believed the alternative worse, and it was I — oh, the loneliness of command — who had to issue the ultimate order, the order we all had the right at that moment to consider one possibly of life or death.

It usually would be safer to ride out a hurricane at sea, but lured by a highly erroneous weather forecast, for which the weather bureau actually broadcast an apology the next day (a first in my memory), we already were so close to shore when the storm struck that I thought clawing our way back out to deep water was likely to be the less successful or, to put it more succinctly, the more dangerous option.

Not exactly comforting was the knowledge that the shoals we were fast approaching had been littered over the centuries with the carcasses of ships whose masters had failed their final crises here. In the eighteenth century wreckers bent on pillage lured captains onto the beach with lanterns. Believing that the lights were other ships in deeper water, unwary captains followed them to their destruction. It was said that the wreckers' children even prayed at night:

"God bless mom and pop and all us poor miserable sinners and send a ship ashore before mornin'."

So there we were, running down on the inlet, the sandy shoals ready to trap us if we missed the narrow channel between the granite breakwaters. The driving rain blinded us as we strained to find those fingers of rock in the wind-driven scud that at times was as thick as fog.

With forty-five to fifty knots of wind blowing directly down that opening and twenty- to thirty-foot waves threatening to send us uncontrollably tumbling down their forward walls, our only course was to tack down toward the channel. But with each tack we lost ground, sideways, toward those breakwaters.

Our situation was about as precarious as it could get when our reefed staysail let go, and a moment later the mizzen sheet parted. That left our engine to do the job.

For ten frightening, seemingly endless minutes, *Wyntje* fought to clear the breakwaters. Now it was just a hundred yards to the comparative safety on the other side of those jagged rocks, but each succeeding wave threatened to crash us down upon them.

And then suddenly, it was done. We skimmed the rocks with only feet to spare and gained the safety of the calmer waters inside the inlet.

Atlantic City is one of the few major inlets along the one-hundred-mile New Jersey coast, and the others, such as Great Egg

Harbor, Barnegat, and Manasquan, can be as treacherous when the following sea is running strong.

When you are seemingly alone out there being tossed about by the wild Atlantic, it is not well to dwell on the fact that only an hour's sail away, right through those inlets and protected by New Jersey's long barrier beach, stretches a huge body of water called Barnegat Bay, and on its marvelously calm waters hundreds of sailboats out of such delightful colonial localities as Waretown, Cedar Run, Forked River, and Toms River are even at that moment cavorting with unworried abandon.

It may be easier for those in the seaside resorts such as Spring Lake and Asbury Park and Bay Head to appreciate something of the ocean sailor's experience, for although they bask on most summer days under their umbrellas on one of the East Coast's great beaches, they too on those stormy days know the Atlantic's uglier moods.

One day more than a quarter of a century ago when we were summering at Allenhurst, I called in an expert for advice on our crum-

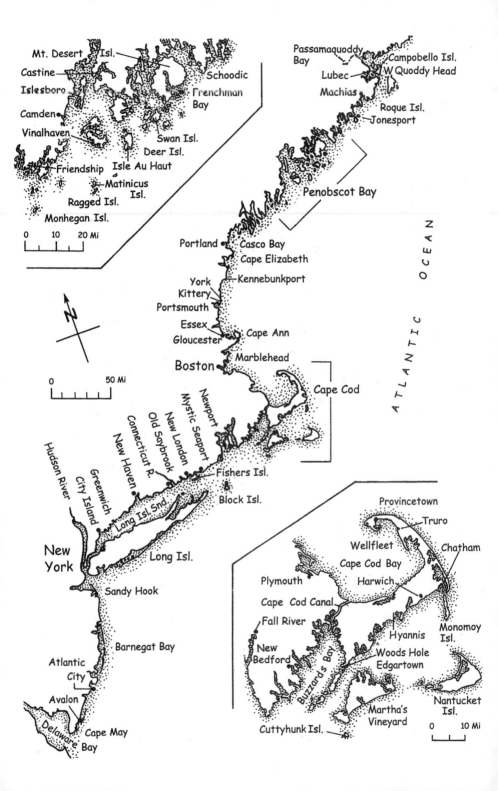

bling seawall. He was a fine old Norwegian who had helped build and maintain many beachfront installations, including, if I remember right, Atlantic City's Steel Pier. He recommended rebuilding the wall, but he said he couldn't guarantee that the new wall would last a week or a hundred years.

"Mr. Cronkite," he said, his pale blue eyes staring out to sea, "I've been at war with that old lady out there for fifty-three years, and I haven't won a battle yet."

Of those New Jersey resorts, the southernmost, down where the shore doubles back up Delaware Bay, is perhaps the most interesting. Cape May is a determinedly antique town that carries off its presumption with uncommon success.

Gasoline buggies with their noxious fumes can choke the most vivid imagination, but despite its summer crowds Cape May almost succeeds in taking one back to the nineteenth century. In its older area most of the homes — the tourist folks say about six hundred — have been either well preserved or restored to Victorian splendor with canopied porches, cupolas, widow's walks, and delicately laced woodwork. At night Tiffany lamps shine through leaded windows.

Congress Hall is still there, still laying claim to having been the first summer White House. President Benjamin Harrison kept an office there when he was a guest at the summer home of John Wanamaker, who was Harrison's postmaster general and the founder of the famous Philadelphia department store.

That was in 1890 and 1891, and Cape May long before had been calling itself the Playground of Presidents. Franklin Pierce, Chester Arthur, and Ulysses S. Grant all vacationed there, and Abraham Lincoln spent a few days there while still a congressman.

The hotel dominates a large beachfront park where John Philip Sousa once led the band concerts and, in fact, premiered a rousing march he entitled "Congress Hall."

Our feathered friends have their own Congress Hall in Cape May, a sort of ornithological Holiday Inn. The cape is directly under the North American flyway, the birds' I-95 to southern climes, and Roger Tory Peterson, the renowned ornithologist, calls it "one of the country's outstanding bird-watching areas." Peregrine falcons, bald eagles, Cooper's hawks, and ospreys drop in for a short stay at its 181-acre migratory bird refuge, and piping plovers, least and common terns, and yellow warblers breed there.

A couple of hundred years ago whales played off Cape May's beaches, and their taking and rendering was a major occupation until the slaughter drove them off. Now tuna and blues are the game, and Cape May's dredged harbor is headquarters of a large fishing fleet, both commercial and sport.

Here at Cape May is where our voyage north-northeast begins, a voyage of more than a thousand miles over open ocean, bays, sounds, estuaries, rivers, and even a fjord, past the wide beaches of New Jersey, the skyscraper canyons of New York, the forested hills of Connecticut, the storied coasts of Rhode Island and Massachusetts, the serrated magnificence of Maine.

For our first leg north, it is too bad we can't take the back road up New Jersey's inland waterway, but its waters are too low for our keel and its bridges too low for our mast, and instead of a leisurely trip through almost unspoiled country of cedar and pine and green marsh grass, we must commit to the fickle Atlantic.

I like to cast off at Cape May in early afternoon, which puts us off Atlantic City about dusk. Just as its gambling towers begin to fade from sight in the gathering darkness astern, we are treated (as we were several times on previous voyages) to a fireworks display celebrating, I suppose, some sinful accomplishment in those dens of iniquity.

Unless the winds turn foul and the seas go wild, this schedule should put us before dawn close enough, perhaps thirty miles away, to see the glow of New York City. The light of a million street lamps in the city that never sleeps tints the sky above and, on nights when the clouds lie low over the tops of the skyscrapers, sets the overcast itself alight with a phosphorescent loom.

Soon—if we have timed it right, just as we turn the corner of Sandy Hook and head up Ambrose Channel toward New York Harbor —the sun will rise back behind us and extinguish for another day those puny artificial lights that a moment before seemed so bright.

And there ahead of us, suspended on a cushion of morning haze, will be one of the most glorious sights among mankind's works on earth. Whatever one's impression of New York City from street level, when seen from this vantage point a dozen miles away across the water, with the sun's morning rays sparkling like jewels off its windows and glass buildings, it is magnificent.

We've put behind us a couple of geological features that played important roles in early maritime history. Mount Mitchill, whose 263-foot height dominates the Atlantic Highlands, once was the first landfall of most of the sailing vessels approaching the North American continent, and most of them anchored in the bight behind Sandy Hook to replenish their water casks from a bubbling well on the Highlands' slope. The watering hole was marked on charts in Spanish, Portuguese, Dutch, and English, and it was known around the world simply as the "Spout."

The sailor who rounds Sandy Hook for the first time without losing a heartbeat or two has no romance in his soul. Sandy Hook is the hinge to America's front door, gateway to the dreams of Emma Lazarus's huddled masses.

The Statue of Liberty might well have gone here instead of fourteen miles up harbor. For more than a century before Liberty's torch was lighted, the lighthouse at Sandy Hook blinked out a welcome to the arriving millions. Although the shifting sands have left it far back from the beach, the ancient building still stands, the nation's oldest operating lighthouse. It was built by the British, and when they left New York in defeat, they were so certain of an early return that they left its light burning.

Not in operation but almost as old is the hook's Fort Hancock. When the sea was our frontier and the skies did not hold our greatest danger, Fort Hancock was part of our first line of defense.

It was the first of a string of forts built originally to protect New York from the British in the War of 1812. Fort Wadsworth on the Staten Island side and Fort Hamilton on the Brooklyn side of the narrows were built after that war was over, but on their sites since the days of the Revolution had been artillery batteries behind earthen barricades.

The most important of these batteries were built at the narrows, that bottleneck where Brooklyn and Staten Island close within a mile of each other before opening out to form New York Harbor. It is crossed now by the Verrazano-Narrows Bridge, which until the British built the Humber Bridge in 1981 was the longest suspension span in the world, beating out the best San Francisco's Golden Gate Bridge can do by twenty feet.

There at the very base of the great bridge's southern tower, grass and ivy growing through the cracks in its granite face, are the impressive remains of Fort Wadsworth. On the opposite shore, under the north tower but almost lost in the mass of Brooklyn buildings, is still-active Fort Hamilton, now a military headquarters compound.

From their locations artillery batteries, as historian Russell Gilmore puts it, "officially opened and unofficially closed the Revolutionary War."

On the very day the Declaration of Independence was signed, the brash young American artillerymen at what is now Fort Hamilton took a couple of potshots at the British warship *Asia.* His Majesty's ship brought her guns to bear and delivered a broadside that practically wiped out the little battery.

Seven years later, the last cannon shot of the war was fired by a departing British ship in soreheaded pique at a group of jeering

Statue of Liberty

American patriots standing on the Staten Island shore.

Those were the last shots ever fired in anger at the narrows. The British didn't dare try to run the gauntlet of narrows' batteries in the War of 1812, and by the beginning of World War II the batteries were so heavily armed that they could have delivered one hundred rounds a minute on an enemy ship.

It was across the narrows that General Howe led his British Redcoats and German mercenaries to attack the upstart Americans in 1776. General Washington's forces were soundly defeated in the Battle of Long Island, but here the general first displayed his military brilliance and conducted the first of what was to be a string of magnificent retreats. The new nation might have ended its days right there if Washington hadn't managed to get most of his army back across the East River to the Manhattan side.

Those forts also played a part in the Civil War, the North using them as prisoner stockades. One of the prisoners was William Henry Fitzhugh Lee, son of the Confederate leader General Robert E. Lee. Ironically the elder Lee, as a captain almost a quarter of a century before, had supervised the strengthening of the very battlements behind which his son was locked.

Ours is a peaceful passage through the narrows, our only hazard the big ships that travel this way. While careful navigation is necessary, this isn't the problem it was only a decade or two ago. The harbor of New York that once was one of the world's busiest is a shadow of its former self. Higher labor costs, cargo containerization, shifting population centers, highways, and airplanes all have contributed to the harbor's demise, and today it seems to the casual sailor that there are scarcely more ships using the port than there were back in 1702, when Lord Cornbury reigned as British governor.

Lord Cornbury set a tone that, as far as we know, no New York governor has lived up to since. He was a transvestite who paraded around New York in his wife's dresses.

The sight of miles of abandoned and crumbling docks that so recently bustled with cargo loading or unloading to or from every port of the world is depressing, but it cannot long divert our attention from the grandeur that remains New York Harbor's.

On her tiny island (which itself was once a fort) the Statue of Liberty continues to reign with new beauty bestowed for her hundredth birthday: her face repainted, her dress redone, her tiara freshly burnished, and her torch restored. And next door on Ellis Island, finally after decades of neglect, the government buildings through which twelve million immigrants passed seeking freedom and fortune in the New World have been spruced up and dedicated as a monument to those newcomers' aspirations. Like the Statue of Liberty, it is now a popular tourist destination.

And right across the broad mouth of the Hudson River is the Battery and Manhattan's southern tip. There is no sight like this anywhere in the world, and it must be seen from the deck of a boat. The great steel and concrete and glass spires tower above you, fighting for space as they reach for the heavens.

Floating out on the harbor's dark waters on a crisp fall night, bundled comfortably against the early chill, the sailor gets another privileged view of fairyland. Dusk comes so early that all the offices are still occupied, and their thousands of lights are on. You are close enough that this great backdrop of light fills your view like a borderless painting. The scene inspires reverential silence.

A little bit of what Manhattan used to be is preserved at the South Street Seaport Museum, on the East River almost under the

Brooklyn Bridge. Some dedicated maritime preservationists have saved
from the wrecker's ball a few blocks of buildings from the early Federal
era, and a redevelopment of the neighboring and equally historic
Fulton Street Fish Market has enhanced the area.

The Seaport's several museum buildings are augmented by two
nineteenth-century sailing vessels, the *Wavertree* and the *Peking.* Their
tall spars overhead and their bowsprits hanging over the cobbled street
below are a small sample of the hundreds of ships that used to crowd
rail to rail for most of a mile from the Battery northward.

Wavertree and *Peking* were not among the largest merchantmen
that once visited New York, but their size impressed us when we
brought *Wyntje* alongside for the first time.

It was a summer day, and a goodly crowd of Seaport visitors
watched our approach with, I assumed, fascination at seeing a real live
sailing vessel coming in from the sea. I had reckoned with the strong
East River current but not with the even stronger eddies along the
wharf front itself, and suddenly, as a collective gasp rose from the spectators above, we were being swept down on *Wavertree.*

I gave *Wyntje* the best help her four-cylinder diesel could offer,
and we just managed to swing free of the *Wavertree's* looming hull, but
now we were so close that our sixty-four-foot-high mast threatened to
crash into the lower of *Wavertree's* spreading yardarms. With the threatening current and the dock behind me, I had nowhere to go but
straight ahead. The flag hoist at the top of our mast just tipped the
Wavertree's yardarm with no damage done.

I swung *Wyntje* to the side of the pier, ordered the lines cast
ashore, and gave a wave to the crowd, intended as nonchalant affirma-
tion that this was the way we always docked. I hope it was only the
sailors among them who could see my heart in my throat.

Traveling up the East River is a whole nautical adventure in itself. For one thing, it is a panorama of modern transportation. We sail under the Brooklyn, Manhattan, Williamsburg, Queensboro, Triborough, Hell Gate, Bronx-Whitestone, and Throgs Neck bridges, the whine of the automobile traffic on the steel grating above providing a deafening ethereal symphonic background for our passage. Subway trains, camouflaged in their graffiti battle paint, rumble overhead, crawling out of respect for the age of the bridges and the rails. Helicopters roar away with their commuter traffic from the riverside pad at Thirty-fourth Street. The swaying cars of an overhead tram carry passengers to the big housing development on Roosevelt (né Blackwell's, né Welfare) Island. Trains carry their intercity passengers and freight across Hell Gate Bridge. Up toward the Long Island end of the river, the big airliners flying to or from La Guardia Airport seem to reach for our mast top as they scream overhead. And most of the way we are accompanied by the cacophony of never-ending traffic on the East River Drive to port.

Back behind that drive stretch the streets of Manhattan. Our water level also is pavement level, and with this peculiar perspective we look down Manhattan's east–west streets. There just beyond the Seaport is New York's first skyscraper, the graceful Gothic Woolworth Building, and behind it the city's currently tallest buildings, the graceless twin slabs of the 110-story (1,350-foot-high) World Trade Center. We pass the vast complex of New York University–Bellevue Medical Center, and down Thirty-fourth Street rises the stately tower of the Empire State Building, long the ruler of this incomparable skyline until the World Trade Center eclipsed it by one hundred feet.

Down fabled Forty-second Street neither tap dancers nor Times Square are visible from the river, but we can see perhaps the prettiest of the skyscrapers, the stainless steel – clad Art Deco spires of the Chrysler Building.

Now comes into view that repository of mankind's still-unrealized hope of a peaceful world order, the United Nations; its broad skyscraper administration building and the sweeping parabola housing the General Assembly almost hang above the riverbank.

Next, just beyond the UN, are some of the city's most luxurious apartments, those of Beekman and Sutton places. We have played long-distance Peeping Toms and searched their windows with our binoculars, but we've never seen any of their famous residents gazing out. On occasional summer days, however, ladies sunbathing on their terraces have inspired presumably irresistible whistles from our younger crew members.

Sutton Place even features some very fancy town houses whose gardens used to run to the river's bank before master developer Robert Moses laid his East River highway there.

On upstream, past the blocks and blocks of Rockefeller University and adjoining New York Hospital, Hospital for Special Surgery, and the Weill Medical College of Cornell University, is another series of expensive apartments surrounding Gracie Square and the lovely Gracie Mansion, built in 1799 and now the home of New York's mayors.

Over behind us to starboard we have left the industrial waterfront of Brooklyn and Queens with its own point of interest— the Brooklyn Military Ocean Terminal, from which almost five million of America's finest shipped out to save democracy in two world wars. Many heroes had their last view of America there.

And the Brooklyn Navy Yard. It laid down the keel of its first ship of the line, the seventy-four-gun USS *Ohio*, in 1817, and 125 years later, during World War II, it was still building, repairing, and servicing much of the Atlantic fleet. Now the historic old yard, like so much of the Brooklyn waterfront, is virtually deserted.

We have made our way up the East River with the current. It is the only way to go. The water runs at up to four knots through here, and it can be a slow passage against it, slow and dangerous. Although the Coast Guard does a valiant job with its large floating "vacuum cleaners" to keep the river clean, occasionally a huge timber breaks off from the decaying docks and, waterlogged, floats just below the surface like a lurking submarine. If a small vessel meets one at any speed, disaster can result, but fatal consequences are far more likely if the boat meets it head-on as it comes sweeping down with the tide.

Just opposite Gracie Mansion, where the Harlem and East rivers join, those fierce currents make up into the treacherous opening called, for good reason, Hell Gate. They tumble and swirl and once in a while form such whirlpools that they can overwhelm a helmsman and capsize a good-sized vessel.

Sailing vessels and the bones of their hapless crews litter the bottom of the river there, but even powerful modern ships have lost to their fury. Only a few years ago, a tugboat was swept below and her crew joined the other Hell Gate victims.

Unless the captain times his passage to make it at slack, sailing through the gate always is a thrill. The current drags at the rudder, the wheel in your hands tugs one way and then another, the bow swings out of path, and, as in driving a race car around a curve, you get the feeling that you are sailing on the very edge of disaster.

Once through Hell Gate and under the Triborough and railway bridges, one has a wider and calmer path for the short run to Long Island Sound. We pass the huge Consolidated Edison power plant (for obscure reasons affectionately known by New Yorkers as Big Alice) and we are at Rikers Island, on which is crowded the New York City prison.

Across from it, on our port, is North Brother Island, with its abandoned isolation hospital to which those with communicable diseases
were banished before the miracles of modern medicine. The hospital
ruins are an unintended memorial to the East River's worst disaster, for
it was here on June 15, 1904, that a burning excursion steamer, the
General Slocum, afire from stem to stern, was run aground as 1,031 lives
were lost, most of them women and children on a church picnic.

We sail on past La Guardia Field, and we are at Throgs Neck and
the twin forts that once guarded the passage between the sound and
the East River route to Manhattan.

Fort Schuyler on our port is now the home of the State University of New York Maritime College, and it is particularly worthy today
of at least one note: In a prizewinning conversion (which one would
like to think was symbolic), architect William A. Hall turned the case-
mates where the great guns once were lodged into a library.

Opposite Schuyler is abandoned Fort Totten, which at the turn of
this century served as antisubmarine headquarters and as late as World
War II was antiaircraft headquarters for the Eastern Defense Command.

Much of our early American history was written on the waters of
Long Island Sound. This inland sea is ninety miles long and up to
twenty miles across, and today it is one of the world's great recreational
boating areas. Authorities figure very roughly that three hundred
thousand boats make their home in the sound's scores of marinas and
clubs, and by far the largest part of them are in that half of the sound
west of Stratford Shoal. Here on any given Sunday in summer it seems
that they all are out, everything from rowboats to princely yachts, in a
chaos of patternless traffic.

Contretemps are as inevitable as on any crowded freeway. There is at least one recorded case of an indignant fisherman who threw crankcase oil over the sail of a yacht that had cut his line. It is a wonder that more serious combat has not erupted. Like opposing nations at war, racing sailors and fishermen alike pray to the same God and both believe He has given them rights to the same spot of water. Happily, shouted deprecations usually to the moment suffice.

Hempstead and Huntington harbors and Oyster Bay and Port Jefferson on the Long Island side and Mamaroneck, Stamford, and Norwalk on the Connecticut side are the largest centers of all this activity, but the queen of them all is venerable City Island. It was a yachting center long before cheap plastics and greater leisure time brought the post–World War II boating boom and before New York City spread its suburban tentacles out along the shoreline.

Politically this twenty-four-block-long, one- to four-block-wide island belongs to New York City, an exotic northern outpost of the Bronx. But spiritually it belongs to the sea and to another age. Until developers discovered it just a few years ago, its neat, middle-class clapboard houses were peopled by those who, like their fathers before them, worked in the boatyards and sail lofts that lined the main street.

Here at yards like Minnefords and Nevins were built many of this century's most famous pleasure and racing yachts. Minnefords itself built four of the vessels that defended the America's Cup.

It was out of City Island Yacht Club that in my earliest sailing days I made my first, tentative forays into Long Island Sound: first just the mile or so out to Stepping Stones Light, and then a mile or so farther to Execution Rocks. Execution Rocks' name came from Revolutionary War folklore, never confirmed by historians, that the British tied American rebels to the rocks and left them for the tide to slowly drown them.

I made all the mistakes in the book, and some not there. Misfiguring the tide and the abating wind, I bounced on the rocks of nearby Hart Island, fearing for the moment that I might join there the uncounted thousands laid in paupers' graves over the last century. On more than one occasion I missed my mooring under sail and, fighting to regain control, ricocheted through the anchored fleet at the club as celebrating members, home from the weekend's races, dropped their drinks and hastened to defend their topsides.

Among those early adventures was my first "long distance" voyage, all of thirteen miles to Greenwich. I spent days planning the trip — food, bedding for the night I would be anchored in Greenwich Harbor, a detailed buoy-by-buoy plot of my course. It turned out it was well that I had taken the latter precaution. The sail up was in a heavy haze, and I could barely see the next buoy ahead. When Greenwich appeared dead ahead through the haze, I dubbed myself Cronkite the Navigator.

The next day, however, the wind had gone northwest and it was breathtakingly clear. As I sailed around the corner of Great Captain Island, which guards Greenwich Harbor, chart in hand to find my way home, there looming on the horizon in front of me was the skyline of Manhattan and, sharply delineated, almost every buoy and rock all the way to City Island. Commodore Walter Mitty stripped Cronkite the Navigator of his buttons.

That summer haze is not an infrequent condition on the sound and through history has shrouded from time to time bloody, nefarious, and heroic goings-on. The earliest colonists depended on their small boats to trade from settlement to settlement, and these often were intercepted by piratical Indians who killed the crews, plundered the cargoes, and seized the boats for further depredations.

These Indians met their match, however, when they ran into a Mr. Tilley, who, according to historian Horace Beck, was "known as Sergeant Kettle because he wore a brass pot on his head in battle." Mr. Tilley may have invented the modern helmet, but it failed to save him the day he was loading hay at Six Mile Island (now known as Nott Island). He and his crew were ambushed and roasted alive.

During the Revolution and again in the War of 1812, the Americans, under cover of haze, fog, or night, slipped out of hiding places along the Connecticut shore, notably the Norwalk Islands, to raid the British on Long Island.

On a hill near Setauket on Long Island, Ann Strong, a member of the Culper ring of Revolutionaries, signaled the colonial whaleboats when it was safe to land. She used her wash line. If the message, for instance, was that the British would not come for two hours, she might hang one set of red long johns and two white handkerchiefs. She varied the articles of clothing and their colors to improvise a code that the U.S. Signal Corps might envy.

It was near there, at Huntington, that Captain Nathan Hale landed by sloop from Norwalk to spy on the British. He was caught and hanged and on the gibbet uttered the words that assured him a place in history: "I only regret that I have but one life to lose for my country."

One hundred and fifty years later there were other strange nocturnal doings in the coves of the Long Island shore. This was a natural center of Prohibition rum-running. Fast, onetime World War I gunboats, now invariably painted black to avoid detection, sped the illicit cargo from freighters lying offshore to beach-side rendezvous from which trucks took it on to slake the nation's thirst.

There were occasional outbursts of gang warfare, shootings, and hijackings on the beaches and roads of then sparsely settled Long

Island, but it was not that which bothered the residents so much. The traffic of the bootleg trucks was so heavy that their more frequent complaint was of the nighttime noise.

Some of the estate owners did note on occasion, however, their annoyance when they would find the otherwise pristine sand of their private beaches cut up by the tracks of beached boats and heavy trucks.

Sailing down Long Island Sound is like voyaging through the pages of *Who's Who.*

Those grand buildings over there at Kings Point off the starboard bow as you sail out into the sound from the East River, over there where all the flags are, where the United States Merchant Marine Academy is now, that used to be the estate of Walter Chrysler, the auto king.

A little farther along are the mansions of the late John Hay Whitney, Otto Kahn, Harrison Williams, Marshall Field, and William K. Vanderbilt, and around the corner at Glen Cove, Long Island, financier J.P. Morgan docked his *Corsair,* the grandest yacht of the many grand yachts that once ran their owners in luxury down the East River to Wall Street in the morning and home in the evening. Now helicopters and seaplanes make this plush commuting run from the millionaires' estates that still dot Long Island's North Shore.

This area was once so resolutely insular in its exclusivity that its socialite residents even developed their own speech pattern, affected by both sexes but particularly favored by the female of the species. It is practiced by speaking with the lips as nearly closed as possible. It can be heard today and is referred to by students of such matters as "Long Island Lockjaw" or, delineating the locale more specifically, "Locust Valley Lockjaw."

Sagamore Hill, which dominates Oyster Bay a bit farther east of Glen Cove, of course was Teddy Roosevelt's beloved home. He rowed the bay's waters with bully enthusiasm and with Mrs. Roosevelt, we are told, as a willing passenger. There is no record that she shared with him an enthusiasm for sailing, a curse visited upon not a few men besides our twenty-sixth president.

This determinedly rustic house of Roosevelt's in the lovely quiet of its tree-rimmed setting seems an unlikely place to stop a war, but there the president negotiated the agreement that, signed shortly thereafter at Portsmouth, New Hampshire, brought an end to the Russo-Japanese conflict. Roosevelt won the Nobel Peace Prize for that.

He shared Oyster Bay with the avid sailors of Seawanhaka Corinthian Yacht Club, one of the nation's oldest yacht clubs and certainly one of the finest on the North Shore. There are not many of the great East Coast yachtsmen who have not picked up its moorings and lifted a cooling drink on its broad veranda.

Directly across the sound, Connecticut boasts its own gold coast of great estates perched royally behind its rocky shore. W. T. Grant, founder of the dollar store chain (that's when a dollar *was* a dollar, young man!), built the big place on the port side as you sail into Greenwich, and right around the corner you pass the gracious home of Victor Borge, with its huge lawn sweeping down to the water's edge. Victor once remarked that it took half of the proceeds from his highly successful concerts just to pay his gardener.

As you head up toward the Indian Harbor Yacht Club, whose big stucco building dominates the harbor, over to starboard and just beyond the club is the mansion where, local legend stoutly maintains, Grover Cleveland had his secret cancer operation in 1893. Actually that successful operation to remove a malignancy from the president's mouth took place on *Oneida*, Commodore Elias C. Benedict's splendid yacht, which was indeed based in Greenwich but at the time of the

surgery was cruising languidly out of reporters' prying reach somewhere on Long Island Sound.

The post–World War II megapolitan spread out from New York
has engulfed most of the Long Island Sound shore, and housing developments, cheek-to-jowl marinas, industry, and oil depots have changed
the character of many of the once unique harbors, but there remain
fascinating cul-de-sacs along the ragged coastline.

In Oyster Bay, anchor at dusk in the shadow under Sagamore Hill
and at dawn take the dinghy in to Cold Spring Harbor. Back up the
road it is a busy suburban city with all the used-car lots and shopping
centers that implies, but down at the waterfront it isn't all that much
changed from its whaling days, the old inn still doing business and
another generation of kids and older folks tumbling into rowboats for
a morning of fishing.

Farther on, the Thimble Islands give the Long Island Sound
sailor a taste of Maine. Two dozen islands, each large enough for at
least one house and a handsome copse of pines and firs, huddle
together in the lee of the Connecticut shore with just enough room for
boats to squeeze between or anchor for the night.

The Connecticut River, which opens into the sound toward its
eastern end, is one of the country's great ecological and historical
treasures. Its waters, which course down from Canada through most of
the New England states, supply almost half the sound's fresh water,
and their meeting with the salt water coming in from the ocean has
created a great salt-fresh-brackish estuary that is a fish-and-bird
nursery of inestimable value. Uncommon and endangered species have
found sanctuary in its protected marshes: the bald eagle and American
bittern, the Atlantic salmon and shortnose sturgeon among them.

Here at the Connecticut's mouth is the only town I know of that was named for settlers who never kept their date with destiny. Back in the early 1600s, a likely spot at the broad entrance to the river was prepared as a place of refuge for Lord Saye and Lord Brooke, who were among the Parliamentarians annoying Charles I with their persistence in seeking constitutional rights. But with the Cromwellian revolution, Saye and Brooke decided they didn't need to flee to America.

"Why should we go through all that colonial bother now?" they might well have asked. "After all, we've already got the town named after us."

So they did, and it has been Saybrook ever since.

Past the broad marshes of the estuary, the Connecticut narrows to wind between forested bluffs, and there as the narrowing begins is Essex, rich in history and a perfect jewel of a preserved colonial city. Up the hill that rises swiftly from the docks great maples, lindens, and evergreens spread their mantles over Main Street and its colonial houses, the whole given even greater authenticity by the continued presence of the gracious old Griswold Inn, opened in 1776 and continuing to do business.

There are two more rivers to explore before Connecticut runs into Rhode Island at Stonington, itself a pretty and historic town, historic if for no other reason than it once was the southern terminus of the railroad from Boston and hence a major transshipping center for the important New York trade.

The Thames River is notable for the fact that we colonials always have defied our British cousins by rhyming it with rain, plains, and Spain instead of with Ben, as in Big Ben, as they do.

The Thames also is notable for harboring a startling anachronism. As you sail up its broad reaches, over to port at the Coast Guard Academy may well be docked the U.S. armed services' only active sailing ship, the beautiful three-masted *Eagle*, while over to starboard at General Dynamics' vast submarine factory almost certainly will be docked the latest of our most modern nuclear submarines.

Around the corner from New London, up through the treacherously rock-studded Fishers Island Sound, is the almost hidden entrance to the comparatively short Mystic River. At its head, barely three miles from the mouth, is the exciting Mystic Seaport Museum, an authentic re-creation of a mid-nineteenth-century whaling village.

Most sailors are romantics, and to sail into Mystic Seaport as the sun begins to set behind the trees that shade the lovely colonial houses on the far shore is one of the most romantic of experiences.

The sun bounces golden off the tall masts of the old whaling ship *Charles W. Morgan*, restored and laying to her stone pier as if waiting for her captain to order another sailing for distant seas. You maneuver in just behind her and warp to a dock from which you can step ashore into another century.

Along the cobblestoned wharf you stride past the blacksmith shop, the barrel maker's, and the printer's to the sail loft and beyond to the old shipyard, where Mystic's fleet of preserved sailing vessels is repaired with the tools and skills of olden days.

And retracing your steps you come back by way of the village's main dirt street, past the dry goods store, the church, and the old pharmacy.

Tied up there at night, the crowd of visitors gone and peace and quiet descended, you share the gathering dark with the ghosts of seafaring generations past. It is an incomparable experience.

Sailing back down the Mystic River and following the channel's tricky turns through an expanse of shallow water, I am reminded of the time a boatload of young people sped past us here, its occupants shouting and waving their arms. I waved back a cheery greeting, and my faithful mate said, "What do you think they were shouting?"

"Why, 'Hello, Walter,' " I replied.

"No," she said. "They were shouting, 'Low water.' "

Such are the pitfalls of fame's egotism.

Back across Fishers Island Sound and past the huge mansions of Fishers Island itself, we sail through the Race, the turbulent corridor where Long Island Sound flows out to Block Island Sound and the Atlantic beyond. We set a course south for the Long Island shore and Shelter Island.

A twelve-square-mile colony of summer homes, Shelter Island is cradled in a curved palm of Long Island, and it invites circumnavigation not only because of the beauty of the passage but also because behind it lies one of the most interesting of all the area's colonial towns, Sag Harbor.

It was a British bastion in the Revolutionary War and the scene of an audacious attack by raiding colonists, it was an American fort and arsenal in the War of 1812 and a base for daring attacks on the British fleet that stood outside, and it was a major port while whaling was in favor.

Remnants of its lush history dot the village, including the cemetery where many of Captain David Hand's wives are buried. The captain was one of the few whalers who survived that dangerous occupation into old age, and he laid away seven or eight wives who did not survive him. He buried them in a row in the cemetery and, the story goes, as he made his way to the docks each morning, he would doff his hat to each of them in turn with a solemn greeting: "Good morning, Susannah; good morning, Mary; . . ."

If the town historian George Finckenor was to be believed, and I certainly didn't doubt him, Sag Harbor continued to the modern day to contribute folk stories to our history. George Balanchine, the great ballet choreographer, is buried in Oakland Cemetery there. On occasional days not otherwise celebrated, a large black limousine drove up. A woman got out. She was slight with muscular legs (a former dancer?) and dressed in black, her face hidden by a heavy veil. She walked quickly to the grave, laid flowers on it, stood with her head bowed for a minute, and left. Balanchine has become to Sag Harbor's Oakland what Rudolph Valentino was to Hollywood's Memorial Park Cemetery.

Sag Harbor has a special place in my memory, a recollection of the day that, caught in a sudden and severe nor'easter, I found refuge there and, having radioed ahead, was met by my good friend the late John Steinbeck, waiting at the dock, wind whipped and rain soaked, ready to give me a hand with the lines.

John sailed those waters with me, full as always of the region's lore, particularly that of Gardiners Island, which lies just off the Long Island shore from Sag Harbor. Surely Gardiners is one of the most fascinating pieces of real estate in all the world.

It is the only estate on the North American continent that is in the fourth century of continuous ownership under the same name. The deed is now held by Robert D. L. Gardiner. His ancestor Lion Gardiner, who had built the fortifications against the Dutch along the Connecticut River, originally bought the land from the Indians in 1639, and then he secured his rights to the property by buying a supplementary deed from Charles I for five pounds.

The island is just under four thousand acres, twenty-seven miles around the frequently rocky, sometimes sandy beach. Gardiners and their servants fought off Indian raids in the early days and, in 1728, repulsed an attack by Spanish pirates that left the manor house in ruins.

By the time of the Revolution the Gardiners were skilled at survival, and they supported both the patriots and the British. In the War of 1812, the British fleet anchored off the island, and its officers were entertained at sumptuous banquets ashore while the Gardiners resupplied the vessels that went on to land the troops that burned Washington.

Long before the Revolution, in the late seventeenth century, the Gardiners and the William Kidd family were good friends with neighboring town houses on Beaver Street in Manhattan. After Kidd took to piracy, he continued to visit his friend's island, and the only authenticated burial place of his ill-gotten treasure was there.

He buried near Cherry Hill twenty-four chests loaded with diamonds, rubies, gold bars, silver, pearls, and East Indian brocades with real gold thread shot through the silk, an Indian mogul's dowry for his daughter. Sailing away he told John, third lord of the manor, "If I come back and the treasure isn't here, I shall have your head or your son's."

Kidd was caught and hanged shortly after, and the treasure was recovered by crown agents. Lord Bellomont gave John Gardiner a detailed receipt for the loot. Two hundred and sixty years later, in 1959, Robert Gardiner received a copy of the receipt the royal household had given to Bellomont when he turned the treasure over to the crown. It was minus six diamonds, which Robert Gardiner assumes Bellomont snitched.

Robert's great-aunt Julia set her cap for the bachelor President John Tyler. Her father, who was a senator, invited her to join the exclusive party on the USS *Princeton*, where the president was to view the firing before Mount Vernon of the biggest gun yet built by the navy. (Shades of a later day, it was called the Peacemaker.) Just before the firing, Julia feigned faintness and asked the president to join her below for a glass of champagne. They were there when the gun backfired, killing the secretaries of army and navy and Julia's father.

"She literally stepped over her father's body into the White House," Robert Gardiner cheerfully recounts, for she went on to marry Tyler and become a powerful influence in Washington, persuading her husband to annex Texas and introducing "Hail to the Chief" as the president's musical signature.

Gardiners Island today boasts a thirty-eight-room manor house, its fourth; 1,250 acres of virgin oak forest; twenty miles of road; an airport; its own power supply replenished by tanker once a year; and a working windmill, the last of five that once graced the fiefdom.

It is home to six hundred swans, six hundred Canadian geese, some one thousand wild turkeys, and so many deer that three hundred have to be shot each year to prevent their starvation. Gardiner, proud that he has maintained the family fortune through shrewd investment, lives most of the time on the mainland in nearby East Hampton, in the home that was John Tyler's summer White House in Julia's day.

Sail east-northeast from Gardiners Island twenty-five miles along the fast-fading Long Island shore, and you come upon a quite different island, named for himself in 1614 by the Dutch explorer Adriaen Block.

Incidentally, Block built his sixteen-ton ship, *Onrust*, on the Manhattan site where, a hundred years later and after some landfill, a black West Indian named Samuel Fraunces would establish the tavern that hosted George Washington's farewell to his troops at the end of the Revolutionary War.

Block Island is a delightfully wild place of steep hills and flower-covered moors dotted with the homes of summer residents. It rises in the south to drop suddenly into the Atlantic, the two-hundred-foot-high bluffs reminding the approaching sailor of the cliffs of Dover. Its broad, protected Great Salt Pond is a popular rendezvous of sailing craft and sleek sportfishing boats that hunt big game — swordfish, tuna, marlin, and sharks — far out to sea.

Once a year it is the scene of Block Island Race Week, which attracts hundreds of sailors for spirited racing and even more spirited hijinks in the broad-verandaed old resort hotels and seafood restaurants ashore.

These are some of the most famous sailboat-racing waters in the world, for it is in the broad Rhode Island Sound between Block Island Sound and Narragansett Bay that the America's Cup was defended every three years from 1958 until the Australians took it home with them in 1983.

The base for those races, of course, was Newport, America's first resort. Its usually pleasant summer climate was "discovered" early in the nineteenth century by southerners who brought first their cotton to its busy port and later their families for the season. The Civil War ended all that, but toward the end of the century, New York society found the place and built the spectacular mansions they demurely called cottages.

Far into this century it was popular to call New York's most privileged society the Four Hundred, for that is the number that Mrs. Astor believed her ballroom would hold. In recent years that limit has been considerably exceeded by those who rent Newport's grand mansions for various entertainments during the America's Cup races.

The Newport Restoration Foundation claims that Newport has more original colonial homes than any other place in the United States, and thanks to valiant restoration efforts led by the tobacco heiress Doris Duke shortly after World War II, the narrow streets running up the hill behind Newport's busy waterfront today are a living and colorful museum of pastel-shaded houses with gambrel roofs.

Sailors of all the seagoing nations trod those streets in centuries past, and even among this generation of the world's racing sailors there probably is no waterfront street better known than Newport's Thames Street, with its jumble of boatyards, chandleries, fish wharves, hotels, and bars — particularly bars.

At least one tavern operating today on Thames Street has known the boots of pirates, privateers, whalers, and merchantmen, and there is the printing establishment founded by Ben Franklin's brother, a headstone-carving shop that has been in continuous operation at the same location since 1705, and Trinity Church, at which George Washington worshiped.

Up the bay a piece from Newport, at Bristol, is the boatyard where the justly famed Herreshoffs thrived.

The blind John Brown Herreshoff founded the yard to exploit the brilliant designs of his brother, Nathanael Greene Herreshoff, an engineering graduate of Massachusetts Institute of Technology. They built everything from the first U.S. Navy torpedo boats to eight successful defenders of the America's Cup, and their work was admired around the world.

Several recent America's Cup contenders have come from the modern Newport yard of Williams & Manchester. The Herreshoffs, the Saunders family across the bay, and others were the progenitors of an industry on Narragansett Bay that today is turning out a large percentage of this nation's pleasure craft.

As we sail out of Newport Harbor to continue our northeast voyage, we pass to port Hammersmith Farm, a notable landmark. Its sprawling white mansion sits at the crown of a great lawn, part of the landscaping designed by the man who laid out New York's Central Park, Frederick Law Olmsted. The owner of Hammersmith at the time, Mrs. Hugh Auchincloss, held the reception there when her daughter Jackie married Senator John Fitzgerald Kennedy.

Here begins the rock-rimmed New England Coast that continues with rare exception beyond the Canadian border, and we must navigate carefully to avoid Brenton Reef, the first of many submerged outcroppings that from now on threaten the unwary mariner.

Reefs named Hen and Chickens, Old Cock, and the Wildcat lie ahead, but we'll leave them well abeam as we make for one of our favorite anchorages, Cuttyhunk Island. A gentle southwesterly, the prevailing wind for summer, boosts us along, and the island will appear shortly through the haze, not a half-day's sail away.

It is well we will reach there early to get the hook down or pick up one of the town's moorings. In summer the little keyhole harbor fills early, sailboats at the deeper end, sportfishermen around the dock at the other.

Cuttyhunk is a cute little nub of a place, essentially one small 150-foot hill on which a few families live year-round, joined each year by a handful of summer people. There isn't much to do, but perhaps that is the point. And anyway, the view from the hilltop is spectacular.

This really is the gateway to a vast 1,800-square-mile vacationland that includes Cape Cod; Martha's Vineyard; Nantucket; mainland communities like Dartmouth, Mattapoisett, and Marion; and the waters of Buzzards Bay and Vineyard and Nantucket sounds that lie in between.

Martha's Vineyard at its nearest point is just four miles off Cape Cod, but it is a world unto itself. Packed into its 108 square miles is incredible topographical, social, and economic variety. Its Vineyard Sound shore is rocky, forested, and framed by bluffs, the spectacular multicolored clay bluffs of Gay Head at the western end. On the Atlantic side there are bluffs, too, but mostly miles of wide, soft beaches and great dunes of sand. Inland there are flat lands of lush farms; ragged, windswept hills; ponds rich in clams and mussels, crabs, eels, snapping turtles; and flocks of ducks and geese feeding on an abundance of wild celery and wild rice.

Its towns are as varied as its land. Edgartown is its showplace, an almost perfectly preserved town of the eighteenth and nineteenth centuries. It was once a whaling port, and the stately captains' houses continue to stand in their white-uniformed grandeur along its treelined waterfront.

Oak Bluffs has its own claim on the visitor's attention. Back in the middle of the nineteenth century, a Methodist meeting ground was built there. A great cone-shaped tabernacle is at its center, and around it, so close together a man can scarcely pass between them, are tiny Victorian cottages, each a gingerbread fantasy.

Most of the village of Vineyard Haven's architectural heritage went up in flames in the great fire of 1883, but the rebuilt town is the island's largest and its commercial hub.

I've always thought Martha's Vineyard deserved more recognition by the cosmetic industry as the possible birthplace of suntan lotion. An early historian noted that the skin of the Indians there was "olive or copper in color, not so much by the science of nature as by the constant application of oil and grease and exposure to the elements."

It was to Martha's Vineyard that Joshua Slocum came in 1902 to retire just four years after completing his famous voyage, the first time anyone had sailed alone around the world.

He chose a farm in West Tisbury, in the island's heart, about as far from the sea as one can get there. His neighbors were other retired sea captains, and it is both a tribute to the island's beauty and a comment on a man's sentiments after a life at sea that so many of them would choose West Tisbury's lovely rolling hills rather than an ocean view.

Slocum kept his equally famous little thirty-seven-foot sloop *Spray* in the nearby fishing harbor of Menemsha, but apparently neither he nor it made much of a splash on the Vineyard. The *Vineyard Gazette* noticed that Slocum had taken up residence with but two sentences, and Captain Donald LeMar Poole, himself an almost legendary fisherman, told an interviewer years later that "not much fuss was made here over Slocum." Poole attributed part of that at least to the fact that Slocum was a merchantman and most of his neighbors had been whalers, and there wasn't much love lost between the two groups.

Perhaps even more important was the simple fact that Slocum was an off-islander. It seems to be a hallmark of New England's island people, perhaps born of a healthy sense of their own permanence of self and place, that they are somewhat suspicious of the transient fame of those who increasingly come to live among them for at least a few months a year.

The famous summer residents on the Vineyard, from the stage, screen, and television and from Wall Street and Washington get no more than the same polite nod from their neighbors and the same cheerful dilatory service from carpenters, painters, and plumbers as the rest of the residents.

This admirable, if unique, sense of values appears in unexpected ways.

At Siasconset, the beautiful village of rose-covered onetime fishermen's cottages on Nantucket's eastern bluffs, the trashman for many years was a courtly Yankee gentleman who bore the good pioneer Nantucket name of Coffin. One morning as on his calls he was having his regular cup of coffee with Marjorie Benchley, wife of the late novelist Nathaniel Benchley, she said to him, "Mr. Coffin, you've known our family so long, why don't you call me Marjorie?"

Drawing himself up to his full dignity, Mr. Coffin replied, "Nevah."

Nantucket's character is vastly different from the Vineyard's. It is more of an "island" island. Smaller than its neighbor eighteen miles away and considerably farther out to sea, it is more unidimensional: flatter, sandier, foggier, and perhaps, for all those reasons, more romantic.

Its major town is also called Nantucket, and befitting its position as once the nation's major whaling port, its captains' houses are made of brick, and they are grandly situated on the hill behind the harbor at the end of cobblestoned Main Street.

To the anguish of conservationists, the town's ramshackle waterfront was rebuilt a few years ago with a modern marina, shops, and restaurants. But the nineteenth-century style of a New England fishing village was retained, and today the area is a major tourist attraction.

I never sail around the Brant Point Lighthouse guarding the entrance to Nantucket's inner harbor without tipping my cap to the ingenuity of our forefathers. Under us there lies a sandbar that should have kept Nantucket from ever becoming the great whaling port it was.

What those old boys did almost two hundred years ago was simply invent a device to lift the heavy whalers over the bar. Called a camel, it was a huge wooden dry dock built in two pieces. It was sunk and fitted around the whaler, the water was pumped out, and whaler and camel were then towed across the bar.

The device kept Nantucket at the top of the whaling business until the whalers, depleting nearby resources, had to go farther and farther to find their prey. Then they needed larger ships, and the larger ships needed a deeper harbor. Thus came New Bedford's moment in the whaling sun.

New Bedford is only eight to ten hours or so by whaler from Nantucket, over on the mainland side of Buzzards Bay. Seldom thought of as a tourist mecca today, New Bedford nonetheless to a sea-loving person is one of the most interesting cities on our northeastern coast.

Its fishing fleet, so troubled in recent years by foreign incursions into waters off the North American shores and the resultant over-fishing, at the turn of the century still consisted of some three hundred vessels, each worth up to a million dollars or more, and together employing around two thousand fishermen.

When New Bedford was the nation's largest whaling port, in the middle of the nineteenth century, more than three hundred whaling ships were registered there, shipping aboard ten thousand men. The city was said to be the nation's richest per capita and its fourth-busiest port.

The decline of whaling began in 1859 with Edwin Drake's discovery of oil in Pennsylvania — a comparatively cheap substitute for whale oil — and the last whaler sailed out of New Bedford in 1925. The decline was speeded during the Civil War when the North bought up the whaling ships, filled them with stones, and sank them to blockade Charleston Harbor.

In its whaling heyday the city, believe it or not, was infested with Pacific Islands cannibals and headhunters. They were inexperienced hands shanghaied by desperate whaling captains who, once safely back home in New Bedford, dumped them ashore.

They inhabited an area known as Hard Dig, a mean, bad, colorful area. And the center of Hard Dig was — what else — a beached whaling ship. It became a bar and brothel called the Ark, the nameplate having

47

been taken off a ship that was being broken up after serving her time faithfully as a legitimate whaler out of Nantucket.

Irate citizens later torched her; the fire almost got out of control and led to the creation of the New Bedford Fire Department, bestowing a unique birthright on that sterling body.

One of the rare occupations of these stranded South Sea Islanders was the sale of shrunken heads, some of which it was said were real but many of which were counterfeit, realistically fashioned out of coconut and rope.

It was in New Bedford that Frederick Douglass lived his first three years as a freed slave and began to establish his reputation as a great lecturer and newspaper publisher.

And among its prominent residents was the wealthy merchant Samuel Rodman, who, among other things, distinguished himself by writing that he didn't think much of young Congressman Abraham Lincoln as a public speaker.

Rodman was one of the nation's early weathermen, albeit amateur. He took weather readings three times a day for thirty years, compiling the country's oldest continuous weather records.

New Bedford's twin city of Fall River also had its place in maritime history as the terminus of the famous Fall River Steamship Line. In the days when railroad travel was still plagued by smoke, cinders, and a lack of air-conditioning, travel by boat was far more comfortable, and the line carried almost half a million passengers a year between New York and Massachusetts.

They traveled in considerable luxury. The great side-wheeler *Commonwealth*, which operated right up until the eve of World War II, was described by the *Vineyard Gazette* at her launching in 1907 as having "a two-deck Venetian-Gothic saloon, a mahogany-and-gold

Empire saloon, and marvel of marvels, an English Renaissance Café high up against the skyline."

One could board the *Commonwealth* or one of her sister ships, the *Plymouth*, *Providence*, and *Priscilla*, at New York's Pier 14 in the evening after work, sail up the East River in the sunset, have a good meal and a night's sleep, and, after transferring to the fast train at Fall River in the morning, be in Boston at 8:40 A.M. What a way to go!

The depression and a seamen's strike forced the folding of the Fall River Line in 1937, and when the great side-wheelers were towed down Narragansett Bay to be broken up in a Baltimore yard, thousands of people lined the shore to bid them, and an era of our maritime history, farewell.

The *Priscilla*'s big steam whistle, an ornately carved newel-post from her grand stairway, and a red plush settee from the main saloon are in the Marine Museum at Fall River, hard by the old Fall River dock and train station.

The steamers of the Fall River Line shared the waters of Buzzards Bay and Vineyard and Nantucket sounds with the great four-, five-, and even six-masted schooners that carried a heavy portion of the coal and timber that moved along our coast right up until the mid-1920s.

They were the last in the great parade of shipping that had grown continuously since the days when romantically named Tarpaulin Cove on Naushon Island was the lair of pirates such as Captain Kidd and Thomas Pound. To guide this commerce through the treacherous waters of Vineyard and Nantucket sounds, some of the colonies' first lighthouses were erected here, Tarpaulin Cove's light in 1759 and Gay Head's, on Martha's Vineyard, in 1799.

Before the building of the Cape Cod Canal, one of the most dangerous parts of their passage was through the swift currents of shoal-ridden Nantucket Sound. The tidal rips around the northeast corner of the Vineyard, an area well named West Chop, are fearsome. When a strong wind, particularly a nor'easter, runs against the three-and-a-half-knot current, the water boils, and right between the Vineyard and Nobska Point on Cape Cod there sits a shallow four-foot spot called the Middle Ground, ready to catch the errant, unwary, or unlucky skipper.

Some Higher Authority with more experience as a skipper than mine must have been watching over me when I first sailed these waters. One lazy day, probably more interested in my guests' conversation than my navigation, I suddenly found that the swift currents had carried us directly over the Middle Ground, and *Wyntje* was saved only by the good grace of its being high tide.

I also have been almost trapped by Horseshoe Shoal, one of the many shallow spots that make of Nantucket Sound a labyrinth not to be assayed by the unskilled sailor in a deep-draft boat. On a hazy day, I lost sight of the buoys and lost track of the current and found the bottom rising to meet the keel. I headed in every direction of the compass to find deep water and was despairing of salvation when the fathometer at last started climbing, and we knew we had broken through.

Fortunately it was a calm day, but I thought of what that predicament could have meant if the wind had been piping up and if we had not had an engine to back up the sails. Not so many decades ago and under just slightly less favorable conditions, Horseshoe would have claimed another victim.

Indeed the records show that in the age of sail, scores of vessels were wrecked each year on Horseshoe, L'Hommedieu Shoal, Hedge Fence, Bishop and Clerks, Halfmoon Shoal, Cross Rip Shoal, the aptly named Wreck Shoal, and the huge complex of sandbars collectively known as Monomoy Shoals, which guard the eastern entrance to the sound and in the distant geologic past undoubtedly formed a continuous landmass from Cape Cod across Monomoy Island to Nantucket.

On one of the area's many sparkling summer days, to the casual layman observing from the shore, the sailboats on bodies of water such as Nantucket Sound appear to be the picture of carefree tranquility. Little does that observer know of the unceasing alertness required and, yes, even of the tension felt by the skippers guiding their vessels through those shoals.

Cape Cod's harbors are almost as tricky to enter as the sound itself is to navigate, but their beauty and that of the towns they serve make the trip worthwhile.

Chatham, at the Cape's elbow, is a charmer, possibly because it seems less commercial than some of the others in this ever more crowded vacationland, but possibly also because its Stage Harbor is one of the most interesting—make that hair-raising—to enter.

One comes in from the sound by threading a needle's eye, a channel barely a boat's width wide and so close to the shore that you can reach out and touch the folks fishing or wading there.

Harwich's entrance isn't much wider, but inside there are three harbors of equal distinction, and just a few miles southwest, if you

Cape Cod Canal

aren't too deep in the keel, there is one of the Cape's prettiest boat trips up the Bass River, winding through a lush countryside of lovely homes, windmills, and inns.

Picturesque Cotuit and Osterville lie on opposite banks of a horseshoe-shaped harbor with islands in its center. Hyannis and Falmouth are the south shore's commercial centers. Hyannis has the Kennedys (Senator Ted and Ethel and the whole tribe are skilled and avid sailors), and Falmouth has a handsome village green surrounded by the familiar houses of ships' captains.

It is in these Cape villages that one can see in profusion, besides the modified saltbox houses that took the Cape Cod name, examples of the gracefully rambling shingle houses first designed by Henry Hobson Richardson, who, as the historians Henry Steele Commager and Samuel Eliot Morison noted, "enjoyed a success greater than any other architect before Frank Lloyd Wright."

Woods Hole, at the Cape's southwestern corner, has several distinctions. It is the home of the world-famed oceanographic institute that bears its name, it is the ferry terminal for the islands, and it overlooks a narrow passage between Buzzards Bay and Nantucket and Vineyard sounds that has terrified skippers since Bartholomew Gosnold first discovered the area nearly four hundred years ago.

The rock-rimmed channel takes almost a ninety-degree turn right in the middle, and when the tide is changing and the current is roaring through at near four knots and the huge buoys are almost buried in the turbulence, the challenge is enough to shiver the timbers of the heartiest sailor.

Just off Woods Hole is Hadley Harbor on Naushon Island, a favorite anchorage for cruising boats. At the end of a narrow twisting passage through huge rocks, it is a scene of bucolic bliss. The Forbes family (of whom the late publisher-adventurer-balloonist-sailor Malcolm Forbes was one) owns the island, and great mansions grace its hilltops like castles on a Scottish moor.

The harbor shore itself, besides the grassy shelf on which horses, cows, and sheep graze, is lined with the support mechanism for an island population — a slip from which the Forbeses' small private ferry runs over to Woods Hole and a boatyard that cares for the family's fleet of pleasure craft.

The gracious Forbeses not only permit anchorage in their harbor but even have set aside one of their small islands on which visiting yachtsmen are invited to stretch their legs.

Hadley's quiet is a welcome refuge on those many days when strong winds whip up the comparatively shallow waters of Buzzards Bay and justify its notoriety as perhaps the Atlantic Coast's roughest sailing ground.

At the other end of the bay, almost landlocked Marion is another popular harbor, a peaceful little inlet with no commerce on its shores, only a hospitable yacht club, a couple of small boatyards tucked away in one corner, and big homes with their manicured lawns running to the water.

Marion is a jumping-off place for the run through the Cape Cod Canal. The eight-mile land cut, dug across the narrow isthmus that joined Cape Cod and the mainland, was completed in 1914, ending a century-long feud between rival interests in the ports of New York and Boston. New York wanted the canal in order to shorten by sixty-five miles or more the route to northern Europe and save sailing vessels the dangerous passage around the shoals of Nantucket and the Cape.

Boston felt that giving New York this advantage would reduce its trade with Europe, but with the coming of faster and safer steamships, Boston lost trade to New York anyway and dropped its objections to the canal.

The Massachusetts Bay side of Cape Cod is lined with historic villages:

Sandwich, where a museum displays examples of the famous glass once made there.

Pretty little Truro, long popular with artists and writers.

Barnstable, one of the towns that sported a liberty pole around which rebellious colonists gathered. Barnstable's pole disappeared one night, and the principal suspect, an outspoken Tory woman named Abigail Freeman, was tarred and feathered and ridden around town in proper style.

And Wellfleet, a summer resort of a very tidy New England nature; the site where Marconi built his first wireless station, which sent his first transatlantic radio message; and once a thriving oyster, cod, and mackerel fishing center. In the 1980s it became the shore station for a diving operation recovering an uncounted treasure of gold, silver, and jewels from the pirate ship *Whidah*, which went down just offshore in 1717, reputedly with the loot from fifty-two ships. Despite scores of searches through the years, the wreckage was not located until 1984.

A few miles or more just out of Wellfleet toward Truro, there is a high sand plateau. From the top you can see most of the Cape and across to Nantucket Sound. It is a part of the northernmost great stretch of beach on the North American continent — forty miles of fine sand that reaches from Nauset Heights, just south of Wellfleet, to Provincetown, on the tip of the Cape. Henry David Thoreau and scores of lesser writers walked that beach; Edward Hopper and scores of lesser artists painted it. Federal protection, local zoning, a short season, and chilly waters have saved it from becoming another Miami Beach.

Provincetown, on the other hand, has not been saved from its own success. The Pilgrims first landed there, enchanted by the wide harbor "wherein," as one wrote, "a thousand ships may safely ride." But they didn't care much for the area, probably because its sandy soil didn't promise the needed crops, and they pushed on across Massachusetts Bay to the place they called Plymouth.

Provincetown was rediscovered in the 1920s by New York artists and writers, who flocked there in such numbers that it was called Greenwich Village North. Mabel Dodge held court there, Sinclair Lewis tarried there, and Eugene O'Neill's first play, *Bound East for Cardiff,* was produced there.

The Pilgrims and the Bohemians came to Provincetown seeking liberties denied them elsewhere: freedom of religion for the one, freedom of expression for the other.

Both groups left their marks on P-town, as its familiars call it. Families of long New England lineage live in some of the Victorian homes in the side streets, while Commercial Street, the main shopping drag, is a summer carnival that smells of popcorn, saltwater taffy, and cotton candy. It is popular with gays, a seasonal Key West North.

Provincetown today also has a comparatively new and thriving industry—whale watching. Every day during the season sight-seeing boats go out a mere seven miles to the Stellwagen Bank, where large numbers of finback and humpback whales spend the summer. Apparently unaffected by the proximity of humans, they put on a spectacular show, breaching and sounding within a few hundred feet of the spectator fleet.

We had an extraordinary experience off the Cape's Atlantic shore a few years ago. *Wyntje* was under power on one of those hazy, hot, windless days without a ripple on the ocean, when suddenly we were surrounded by whales. Appearing above water and then diving again, they were impossible to count, but it seemed that there were scores of them as far as the eye could penetrate the haze.

At one point two of them bracketed us and swam alongside not a hundred feet away. I think they were fins. They were longer than our forty-two-foot boat, certainly big enough to unintentionally swamp us.

They were with us for perhaps half an hour before we left them behind. And then within a few minutes we just as suddenly were surrounded by dolphins, and now it seemed there were hundreds of them. First one pair and then another would come alongside to pay us a visit and play around our bow. As always with these delightful creatures, we regretted the moment they decided to say good-bye.

It is twenty miles, barely a half-day's sail, from Provincetown across to Plymouth, the last stage of the Pilgrims' two-month voyage from England. Whether that sick and weary band really scrambled ashore across what is now called Plymouth Rock is questionable, but unquestioned is that the rock is a tourist mecca. The proof is that people throw coins at it. One of nature's mysteries is why tourists throw coins at any small body of water they can look down upon — fountains, wells, fishponds.

Docked nearby is a life-sized replica of the Pilgrims' *Mayflower*, and it is worth a visit to appreciate the discomfort suffered by those 102 souls crammed on its tiny deck and packed into a common cabin with barely room to stand. No matter what they thought of Provincetown, it is a wonder that once they were ashore anything could have persuaded them to climb back aboard that floating prison.

Pleasingly colonial Duxbury, two miles across Plymouth Bay, almost certainly was the nation's first suburb. It was founded by some

Constitution

of the Pilgrims who fled the growing "urbanization" of Plymouth. Today, with Scituate and Cohasset, it is one of the chain of harbors favored by Boston yachtsmen.

The American who can sail into Boston Harbor without feeling embraced by history has no feel for history at all. The imagination runs riot as you approach the almost legendary land of those places of our nation's beginnings, even though you can't really see them from the water anymore. Bunker Hill has been cut down and hidden behind tall buildings; Griffin's Wharf, where the tea was dumped, has disappeared under landfill, as has the dock where John Hancock's ship *Liberty* was seized by the British, touching off some of the earliest rioting.

The *Constitution*, "Old Ironsides," is there though, venerable reminder of our great seafaring heritage, veteran of the 1812 battles that conquered the vaunted British and brought forth a new power on the world's oceans.

Once a year, on July 4, she is towed away from her dock at the old Charlestown Navy Yard and out into the harbor, turned around, and towed back, the exercise to keep her from weathering on one side only. The Navy and the people make a big ceremony of it, as they should. The old girl is adorned with flags as she might have been when she sailed out to meet the *Guerrière*, and on her quarterdeck a band plays.

A fleet of horn-tooting spectator boats falls in alongside, and cheering, flag-waving crowds line the shore. At noon there is a salute from the *Constitution*'s antique guns, specially reinforced for the occasion. And across the harbor old Fort Independence's cannons, firing in honor of the holiday, seem to return the salute. It is enough to bring tears of appreciation to an old salt's eyes.

Boston was the first of the northeastern ports to renovate its run-down waterfront; today the Constitution and Lewis wharves have been rebuilt, and one can dock for the night almost under the restored market hall that merchant Peter Faneuil gave to the city in 1742.

Intrigued by the grasshopper symbol of the Royal Exchange in London, Faneuil had a large grasshopper placed over the cupola of his building. In the War of 1812, the grasshopper became a password on the waterfront. Anyone who didn't know that it was a symbol of Boston was suspected of being a spy.

A couple of hours' sail out of Boston and the imagination can rest as one picks up a mooring in the crowded harbor of Marblehead. In contrast to Boston's, its waterfront was remarkably untouched by the twentieth century.

Some of the old houses tottering on the winding streets go back to the days when Captain Samuel Trevett marched the Marblehead company out to do battle at Bunker Hill. The Lafayette house is so named because a corner had to be cut away to permit the Marquis de Lafayette's carriage to navigate the turn. There are a few bars that evoke the days when "one for the road" frequently turned out to be the Mickey that delivered the unsuspecting patron to a shanghai gang and a long term of servitude at sea.

It is no wonder that this picturesque and lively port has become a favorite of the international yachting fraternity and the principal sailing center of the Boston area. With three major yacht clubs on its shores, it also is one of the most crowded harbors on the East Coast and, when the wind goes around to the northeast, one of the roughest.

Many a night, as a strong nor'easter began to bounce the fleet about, we pulled our foul-weather gear over our pajamas and got underway to make a cold and uncomfortable run the four miles to a haven under the lee at Manchester across the bay.

Around the corner from Marblehead is Salem, which as early as 1664 was referred to by a colonial scribbler as noted for its "rich merchants" and its gabled houses. One with seven gables was made famous by Nathaniel Hawthorne, others for harboring the Salem "witches" or those who condemned them.

Salem's golden years of international trade came immediately after the Revolution when it had 252 vessels in commission, most of them sailing to India and China in a trade developed by one Elias H. Derby. He successfully defied the monopoly until then held by the East India companies of the Dutch and the English and became America's first millionaire.

Old Derby Street Wharf is still there, and you can put your boat alongside and tie up where Elias's vessels used to be more than two hundred years ago.

Along the twelve miles of rugged coast from Salem to Gloucester, in such communities as Beverly, Prides Crossing, Manchester, and Magnolia, is a mixture of old colonial houses and mansions of this century. Sailing the route up the Cape Ann coast, one does well to steer wide of Norman's Woe Reef. It is there that Henry Wadsworth Longfellow's doomed ship *Hesperus* wrecked.

Gloucester was founded in 1623 as a fishing port, and a fishing port it has remained to this day, generations of its men working the rich Georges Bank a hundred miles or more offshore. If it was not already famous, Spencer Tracy, Lionel Barrymore, and Freddie Bartholomew made it so with the 1937 movie *Captains Courageous,* which graphically depicted the hard life of the deep-sea fishermen. With startling modern technology an even more graphic representation came along in 2000 with the film *The Perfect Storm.*

Like New Bedford's, Gloucester's fishing fleet has fallen on hard times in recent years, but through it all the imposing statue of the Gloucester Fisherman stands at the waterfront, his eyes fixed on the ocean that is his life.

Rockport, Gloucester's suburb on the Cape's side, is an artist colony overrun by tourists, most noted for its red fisherman's shack that has been the subject of so many paintings that it has become known as Motif Number One.

In 1713 Gloucester gave the world the practical sailboat known as the schooner, but it was at Essex, north of the Cape at Ipswich Bay, that most of the finest Gloucester schooners were built. The yard now is a shipbuilding museum.

The Massachusetts coast runs out just beyond Newburyport, even as that town's fame and prosperity as a major port went out with the clipper ships. In recent years, however, its downtown area has been renovated, and experts on Federalist period architecture say its old captains' houses on High Street are among the finest examples to be found anywhere.

New Hampshire's little window on the ocean is an eighteen-mile stretch of coast most notable for the harbor of Portsmouth, a major shipbuilding center in the nineteenth century. Upriver, in the days of wooden ships, ninety sawmills cut the trees from New Hampshire's lush forests into nine million feet of lumber a year to build a good part of America's merchant marine. Today a naval shipyard continues to be active at Portsmouth.

Visible from some miles at sea, at the entrance to the Piscataqua River, is the seemingly endless expanse of one of the country's finest old Victorian hotels, Wentworth-by-the-Sea. You can sail right up to its broad grounds and nestle for the night along the shore where the Russian and Japanese diplomats probably strolled between sessions of their peace conference back in 1905. The treaty ending the Russo-Japanese War, the one engineered by Teddy Roosevelt back there at Oyster Bay, was signed at Portsmouth.

From the Wentworth on a clear day you can see the complex of nine small granite islands ten miles out to sea known collectively as the Isles of Shoals. It is an adventure to sail among them, following an otherwise almost unmarked path between the great slabs of gray rock. And, if the timing is right, fields of orange-red poppies crown the bare hills like a May wreath on a bald head.

Almost from the moment of their discovery in 1605, the isles were a major rendezvous for fishermen from all over Europe. An early historian recorded:

> Fishing vessels came hither . . . Doggers and Pinckies of the
> English, clumsy Busses of Holland, light Fly-boats of Flanders,
> the Biskiner and Portingal and many other odd high-peaked
> vessels were attracted thither summer after summer.

Governor John Winthrop noted in 1634 that the isles settlement's assessed property was equal to that of New Plymouth, and as many as seventeen fishing vessels arrived from Europe in the single month of March.

The islands' serious modern development came in 1848, when one Thomas Laighton established a resort there and became keeper of the lighthouse.

Despite, or maybe because of, the isolation and even bleakness of the place, the resort was something of a success, and by the time Laighton's daughter, Celia Thaxter, was making her mark as a poet toward the end of the century, it had become the summer rendezvous of musicians, painters, and writers, Oliver Wendell Holmes and John Greenleaf Whittier among them.

The Thaxter home was on Appledore Island, now the site of a marine research laboratory. The successor to Laighton's resort, a large white frame structure on smaller Star Island, is now a church-run conference center.

Maine begins on the banks of the Piscataqua at Kittery, where in 1777 the first warship commissioned by the fledgling U.S. Navy was launched. Under the audacious command of John Paul Jones, the *Ranger* a year later was sailing in and out of British ports, torching the ships it found and terrorizing the locals.

From Kittery to Portland the Maine coast is marked by a trio of keyhole harbors, York, Kennebunkport, and Cape Porpoise, each with its own distinction for the sailor.

Built-up York is tricky to enter — a sharp right turn and a couple of rocks marking a narrow channel. At artsy Kennebunkport it is worth waiting for high tide to get over its shallow entrance. Picturesque Cape Porpoise has so many lobster traps at its entrance that it almost defies entering at all.

Cape Porpoise was the first Maine port into which I sailed uncounted years ago, and I learned two unforgettable lessons that day: first, running over a lobster pot can ruin your whole day, and second, going overboard to cut it loose from your propeller is an exercise only a masochist could enjoy. No warning is strong enough to indicate how cold Maine waters really can be in June.

Just before turning Cape Elizabeth for Portland, one can sail up to the resort community of Prouts Neck for a quick visit to the modest house where Winslow Homer painted many of his famous seascapes.

Portland's waterfront, a few years ago a disaster area, has been faithfully restored as part of the city's vigorous redevelopment program. The old cobbled streets at the docks now lead up to several blocks of ancient mercantile buildings housing coffee shops, restaurants, and boutiques.

There are those who will tell you that as you sail out of Portland you finally have reached the "real Maine." Others will claim that the "real Maine" begins somewhere farther east. This is part of a Mainiacal one-upmanship practiced by cruising sailors who find that part of the joy in voyaging is going somewhere others have not.

The only way to beat their game is to sail off the Maine chart into Canada, but the truth is that the sailor's Maine, the "real Maine," is right there out of Portland Harbor where Casco Bay begins.

Maine is a sailing paradise, and the roughly 240 square miles of Casco Bay, dotted with its 365 islands, offer a sampler of its joys. The cool air is so clean that a city dweller's lungs want to burst with the marvel of it; the water is so clear you can see the lobsters scurry over the bottom; the winds rise on most days to take you on silent wings of canvas to new delights.

A daylong voyage from Portland through the labyrinth of Casco's islands brings us to one of my favorite anchorages, and for a first night it holds the promise of so many more just like it to come. It lies off the bay down a narrow corridor between the rocks, with the dark green spruce and cedar forming overhead a canopy that almost shuts out the summer's bright sun.

Inside, the passage opens into a small lagoon, the corridor is swallowed by the trees, and we seem to be alone on a lake suspended in space and time. The splash of the anchor is an intrusion. A loon, watching from the near shore, takes its leave with a crazy cry.

The air is warmer here, away from the ocean winds, and a test of the water even invites a swim — brief, but a swim. From the cockpit, the evening libation in hand, we watch the fish ripple the water as they pursue their evening meal.

A pair of ducks appear from nowhere, and we dive below for the bread we've saved for this occasion. Soon our apparently grateful ducks are joined by half a dozen sea gulls that, with unexpectedly good manners, hang back and wait for second table.

The smell of our dinner on the galley stove doesn't fight, but rather complements, the sweet sunset fragrance of the damp forest, and it foretells an evening around the table with good talk and good wine and the overhead kerosene lamp warming us with its soft glow.

Abed, under a blanket or two, we're sent to sleep by a gentle wind just strong enough to ripple the water against our hull and speed a whisper through the trees.

We'd have to get up mighty early to enjoy a morning as peaceful as the night, for dawn brings the lobstermen and their chugging engines and the radios they play at maximum volume so they can hear them over those engines.

The lobstermen and their efficient little craft are everywhere in Maine waters, and as we sail on down east and the day grows longer, we'll be hailing one of them to buy some of their fresh catch, and the evening will find us partaking of one of the sea's greatest gifts to mankind.

Not everybody, it turns out, likes lobsters. They are the only thing about Maine, as nearly as I can make out, that one of our late dear friends and sailing buddies, television's Gary Moore, didn't like. He refused to eat them. He called them "seagoing cockroaches."

There will be other anchorages similar to our first and some others of equal charm but different character. There are the bigger towns (although none in Maine are very large) such as Boothbay Harbor, Camden, and Bar Harbor with their busy, crowded waterfronts and their charms almost buried under summer tourists. Camden is home port for the windjammers that take the venturesome for one-week cruises and bring to Maine's waters a touch of days past.

Maine Coast Lobster Boat

Northeast Harbor demands a stop, gateway as it is to Mount Desert Island and Frenchman Bay and, with its superbly run municipal marina, in its own right a worthy destination.

Around the corner is the deep fjord known as Somes Sound, and at its head is one of Maine's prettiest harbors. A narrow keyhole is its entry. Spectacular homes cantilevered over the rocks adorn one shore, and Mount Desert's oldest town, Somesville, sits delicately on the other.

Somes Sound Harbor is an example of the Maine harbors of limited facilities but unique attractions. I'm thinking particularly of Christmas Cove, up the Damariscotta River a short distance above Linekin Neck, where Mike Mitchell and his family, refugees from Madison Avenue, run a restaurant that has become a mandatory stop for cruising yachtsmen. Christmas Cove was given its lovely name by the peripatetic Captain John Smith, who — guess what? — spent Christmas Day there in 1614.

Special, too, is Castine up in the northeast corner of Penobscot Bay. It nestles on the side of the hill looking down on its natural harbor, its main street climbing past the one-junction business section to the brow of the hill and the neat, green campus of the Maine Maritime Academy. The academy's big training vessel, a troop transport ship used in the Korean War, rests much of the year next to the town dock.

It sits not far from where the young American navy suffered one of its worst defeats of the Revolution, an unsuccessful attempt in 1779 to drive the British from Castine.

Castine was heavily loyalist in the Revolutionary War, and when its residents learned that the boundaries of the new nation included them they took down their houses, board by board, loaded them on scows, and towed them across the new boundary, the St. Croix River, to St. Andrews, on the "safe" side of Passamaquoddy Bay. Their descendants are there today.

Very special are the little harbors with one- or two-store villages (if, indeed, there are any stores at all) where the summer people moor their boats alongside those of the working lobstermen. Sorrento is one we are fond of, where there is nothing ashore but comfortable homes, hospitable friends, and a long walk to the highway, and where one night we lay on the deck until dawn watching the heavens fill with an incredible display of the aurora borealis.

Another anchorage is a favorite of ours not only for its beauty but more particularly for the friends there. Russell Wiggins and his wife, Mabel, were natives of Minnesota but became as much a part of Maine as if their ancestors had settled there a century or two ago.

Russell bought the Ellsworth *American* in 1966 when he retired as managing editor of the *Washington Post*. With his meticulous editing, his high reportorial standards, and his own editorials and particularly splendid verse on everything from human follies to the beauty of a Maine winter, he turned it into perhaps the best weekly newspaper in the country.

Their lovely, sprawling old farm home on the banks of the Benjamin River at Brooklin became a mecca for their hundreds of friends from across the country — partly because of Mabel's infectious good humor, but also to no small degree because of her irresistible three-bean salad and blueberry pies. Into his nineties Russell sailed his beloved Friendship sloop. Built in 1904, it was believed to be the second-oldest of this venerable Maine boat in existence. He sailed it, alone much of the time, up and down the Maine coast, pursuing his insatiable quest for local lore.

His unflagging high spirits usually broke through the Yankee reserve of his neighbors, but not always. He told of the day he was sailing up to an abandoned stone pier in a little-used harbor. His approach was watched silently by an old-timer standing on the dock looking for all the world like the model of those kitsch wooden figures you can buy at any New England souvenir stand — the Maine (or Gloucester or New Bedford or Nantucket) fisherman with his gray beard and his yellow hat and coat and boots. Suddenly Russ fetched up hard on a rock barely fifty feet from the dock.

"I've gone aground," Russ yelled to the old-timer.

Removing the pipe from his mouth, the old-timer answered, "Thought ya would."

Around the corner from the Benjamin River, up Eggemoggin Reach, one can find the ruins of one of the ice factories that in the nineteenth century shipped Maine ice around the world. Cut in huge pieces from freshwater ponds in the hills above the reach, the ice was lowered by railway to a stone dock below where large sailing ships waited for the valuable cargo. Packed in sawdust in the hold and naturally cooled by the ocean waters outside, enough survived the long trip to provide luxurious Maine ice even for the British colonists in India.

Ice was a big Maine export in the days before electric refrigeration, taking its place just slightly behind timber, shipbuilding, and fishing as a major industry.

Back up the tree-lined road along the coast behind the Wigginses' house is an unprepossessing clapboard church with a modest steeple where the visiting yachtsman, if fortunate enough, can experience an exciting evening of Americana.

At irregular intervals and apparently inspired just by the whim of a member, an evening sing is organized. A simple hand-lettered cardboard sign posted on the fence in front announces the event, and on the appointed evening the church fills early. The leader calls out the number of the first tune, and the assembled audience seems to know the number and the words so well that its members scarcely need the hymnals in front of them. After the first selection, they call out the number they would like to do next, and it is done.

It strikes one, in this environment where so many of the participants earn their living from the sea and have seen so many kin go down to it never to return, how many of our American and British hymns have a nautical flavor.

At Lash's yard in Friendship, you can have one of the handsome little sloops like Russ's built on order. Friendship is a pretty village perched above a working lobster harbor, and Lash's Boatyard sits on a curve of the road just outside of town.

A visit there is something of a disappointment, or perhaps, in the unpretentious milieu of Maine, it should be called a pleasant surprise.

Friendship sloop

Totally unmarked by a sign of any kind, it is a big, weathered shed that threatens to slide down its own railway across the rocks to the water below.

On our last visit there we found the doors wide open but not a soul inside. There was an old powerboat apparently in for repairs. Tools were lying about, half covered with sawdust. Most of them looked as if they had come from an antique exhibit at a marine museum, but we knew they were the instruments of artists.

In the town of Friendship a sign notes the mileage to some other Maine communities. It says, "Freedom 45; Liberty 33; Harmony 96; Unity 52; Union 20; Hope 27. Friendship is here."

There are Maine historians who take some umbrage at the attention given Plymouth as the first settlement on the American shore. Though acknowledging that the intended permanence of the Plymouth Colony bestows its uniqueness, they point out that many fishing camps were established by the British, Portuguese, Dutch, and others in Maine some years before Plymouth was founded, and many of these had the character of permanent villages.

In fact, they note the camps were so well known that in their first, terribly hard winter the Plymouth colonists sent a boat up to Maine to buy fish to tide them over.

Most of those early fishing camps were on the islands that pepper the waters off the Maine coast — forbidding and mostly barren rocks of various sizes; some, those without natural harbors, uninhabited; others, where there is some shelter into which to bring a boat, with a half-dozen or a dozen hardy families who year-round eke out a living from the sea and send their children by boat across miles of open sea for schooling.

The larger islands, such as Monhegan, Isleboro, North Haven, and Vinalhaven, now host large communities of summer residents. Monhegan has been popular with several generations of noted artists.

Rockwell Kent's old home is now that of Jamie Wyeth.

One of my favorite Maine scenes is Ragged Island — barely a mile long, one of the smaller outcroppings of rock that can sustain life. Its tiny harbor has an entrance that, if not in configuration at least in difficulty of entry, is typical of the islands. It is barely a boat length wide, and hidden rocks guard the shores. When the wind is from the north and the sea is making up, it is a dangerous entry, and even under ideal conditions on a lovely, fog-free summer day, the ocean surge threatens to lift the unwary yachtsman out of control onto those feared rocks.

Inside, the harbor is cozy but crowded with the dozen or so lobster boats that make this home.

Like some giant's backyard fishpond, the almost circular harbor is lined with granite boulders. The only access to shore, unless one wants to chance rowing one's dinghy up on those rocks, is via the wooden dock that reaches out into the harbor. As with all of the piers in this part of the world where the tides run fifteen feet or more, at low tide its spindly structure seems to defy gravity. The climb from the boat below up its perpendicular wooden ladder is not for the fainthearted.

It seemed almost too crowded for *Wyntje*'s forty-two feet when first we sailed into Ragged Island Harbor; maneuvering was tricky and uncomfortable in the little basin and made particularly difficult by the long mooring lines that the lobstermen had stretched across the harbor.

A young lobsterman unloading his boat of the day's catch saw our dilemma and, waving to one of the moorings ahead of him, shouted, "Pick it up. He's gone to Rockland. Won't be back tonight."

We gratefully accepted the offer and were lying comfortably to the line when the tide began to fall, and a huge rock began creeping into view under our stern. The tidal fall stopped as we had but inches between us and impalement.

So precipitous are some of the harbor's rock ledges that the depth sounder in the center of the boat, as in our case, might show plenty of water while there is none off either end.

From the dock appears one of those visual vignettes that constantly delight the visitor to Maine. With the tide running out, the long mats of seaweed flow back and forth into beautiful patterns of green between the rocks, as if some celestial surrealist were playing at his palette.

Past the modest houses of the lobstermen nestled around the harbor, one climbs up over the hill to see stretched below the whole breadth of the Atlantic, the waves it generates off Portugal finally fetching up on Ragged's rocks with a crunching assault that appears to threaten to push the tiny island off its granite base.

Part of Ragged Island's charm is in the derivation of its name. Some Maine historians such as Charles B. McLane assume that it can be traced back to the Abnaki Indian name for "island rocks," *raggertask*. From this came the British seaman's natural translation to "ragged ass."

That gave way to the more colloquial "ragged arse," and, indeed, as Ragged Arse it was shown on the pre-Revolutionary charts. It is still called that by lobstermen of the area, although mapmakers of Puritan bent in the early days of the Republic charted it as simply Ragged Island. That name sticks, but officially it has been Criehaven, after a founder, since its 1896 incorporation.

The chain of larger islands forms a virtual gold coast of wealthy summer homeowners. Rockefellers, Astors, Morgans, Vanderbilts, and scores of others of almost equal fame populate the area in July and August. They all seem to play a game of one-upmanship as to who has been coming to Maine the longest, although most of them count their years there in generations. And their traditions run deep.

In the 1880s the rich vacationers on North Haven commissioned a local shipwright named J. O. Brown to build them a fifteen-foot day sailer they would call the North Haven dinghy. Now, more than a century later, the North Haven dinghy continues to be raced in the Penobscot Bay waters off North Haven, probably by grandchildren and great-grandchildren of the original owners. And the third generation of descendants of J. O. Brown are building boats there today.

North Haven's twin island of Vinalhaven (they are separated only by the busy channel known as Fox Island Thoroughfare) has its share of well-to-do summer people, but I like to think its greatest fame is that the Carvers, who gave their name to Carvers Harbor, were probably the world's biggest horsenet manufacturers. Horsenets kept flies off horses, a matter of concern to a considerable population of horses at one time.

According to Bill Caldwell, Portland *Press Herald* columnist and author of innumerable books on Maine lore, more than a thousand persons worked for the Carvers making horsenets not only on Vinalhaven but at Port Clyde and on Deer Isle. Of course, Henry Ford put a stop to all that.

The Maine islands were the subject of great real estate speculations as early as Revolutionary times, and Caldwell tells the tale of the most fascinating of all the speculators.

Colonel James Swan is a much overlooked figure of our early history. He was a Revolutionary War hero, an abolitionist half a century before his time, and a dreamer who envisioned an empire of prosperous islands of which one that he modestly named Swan's would be the centerpiece.

His dream collapsed, and he fled to Paris to escape his debts. There he raised money for the young American Republic but once again overspent, this time ending up in debtors' prison. For twenty-two years he lived, rather than languished, in prison. Using funds sent him by his wife in America, he sponsored lavish parties for his French friends outside the prison. Of course, he himself could not attend. He asked only that an empty chair be held for him at the head of the table and that a toast be drunk to him.

Out to sea away from Ragged Island is an even smaller island, so small, in fact, that it is only called a rock — Matinicus Rock. There are no people on it, but thousands of tourists come to visit its inhabitants each summer. They are the Disneyesque little birds known as puffins, colorful Harlequins in their bold black-and-white plumage with white face and breast, bright orange webbed feet, red-ringed eyes, and beaks with a blue base, tipped in orange.

They come to Matinicus to breed for a few weeks each year. They are scarce, and landing on the island, even if its sharp cliff would permit, is discouraged. But this is hardly necessary anyway. On a calm day they swim surprisingly close to your boat. When they catch a fish, you get a good view of them, their struggling meal clasped in their beaks, making a quick reconnaissance flight along the cliffside before suddenly disappearing into the particular crevice where they nest.

Speaking of birds, fall is a wonderful time to sail almost anywhere but is particularly rewarding in Maine. Although its waters are never really crowded, by fall almost the last summer sailor has gone. One can sail all day without seeing another boat, and the anchorages are delightfully empty.

But a special bonus is the geese and ducks rafting up, organizing, getting their orders, it seems, for the migration south. It fills a human with envy to know that they will make their trip without listening to an interminable concert of canned music while waiting "for the next available reservation clerk."

Every winter as we sail south and watch in admiration as the great flights of geese pass overhead in the V formation, a veteran of our crew, Fred Celce, asks the newcomer, "Do you know why one side of the V is longer than the other?"

"No, why?" asks the innocent freshman.

"More ducks," says Celce.

The islands of Maine are frequently in such clusters that they form an intriguing mystic maze that would draw the admiration of a puzzle maker or a British gardener.

Once we sailed from Martha's Vineyard directly to Maine, making our landfall as planned at the southwestern corner of Penobscot Bay for a rendezvous with Mike Forrestal on his *Belle*. Mike had been sailing those waters all his life and knew them intimately. At the appointed hour he radioed for our position. I gave it to him and remarked that his radio transmission was coming in good and strong.

"It ought to be," he replied. "I'm about five hundred yards from you, just on the other side of the island you are now passing to port."

The British navy and American privateers played hide-and-seek here, and down through history, to this very day, smugglers have island-hopped their illicit goods past harried government agents.

It was in the knot of little islands off Stonington that Charles and Anne Lindbergh found seclusion for their honeymoon. They slipped away from the summer estate of her father, Dwight Morrow, on North Haven and sailed to a lovely cove on McGlathery Island as the newshawks searched frantically for them.

Navigation among the islands is tricky enough on clear days, but it can be harrowing on those frequent days of fog. It may come in on cat feet as Carl Sandburg insisted, but it has the viciousness of a mother tiger at bay.

A Maine fog can come up in minutes with smothering density. The bow of your boat and the top of your mast disappear, and you are cast adrift in an impenetrable sea of white.

However, the old-time sailors in Maine, and particularly the lobstermen, go plunging about in the fog with unearthly ability to find their way. I asked a lobsterman how in the world he did it.

"How do you know where the rocks are?" I asked.

"Don't," he answered. "I know where they ain't."

A fellow yachtsman tells of asking the same question of a lobsterman. His answer was somewhat different.

"Why," he bragged, "I know every rock in Muscle Ridge Channel." With that the lobster boat bounced off a submerged rock.

"There's one now," continued the lobsterman, without missing a beat.

That might have been Wiggins Rock, which Russ Wiggins insisted was not named for him. If you are a sailor, it is not a good thing to have a rock named after you.

Of course, the modern miracles of navigation, radar, and loran have taken much of the danger out of the fog, but care still is needed. The radar set on *Wyntje* is below in a conveniently darkened navigation room, and the radar operator, usually me, communicates to the helmsman in the cockpit by radio.

My wife and one of my favorite companions, Bill Harbach, have a lot to live down for their treatment of their captain on one foggy day as we were sailing around Mount Desert. I was below calling up instructions:

"All right, steer 265 and you have a buoy about one-quarter mile ahead." A pause. "Okay, do you see the buoy?"

"Yep," Bill would answer. "Right on it. What next?"

"Steer 287 — a black buoy another quarter of a mile."

This went on for half an hour or so when, at an open stretch of water, I chose to get a breath of fresh air above decks. I emerged into bright sunlight!

"When did the fog clear?" I asked in amazement.

"Oh," Bill innocently replied, "about twenty minutes ago."

A summer visitor at Bass Harbor took a small boat out on an average Maine day, only to be helplessly lost in the fog. He came ashore on Great Gott Island and called for help: "Is there anyone here? Is there anyone here?"

Mrs. Gott heard his cry at her house on the hill and came down through the fog to the rocks below to find her unexpected visitor standing beside his boat.

"May I introduce myself?" he said. "I'm Admiral Byrd."

So famous was he then, he did not need to identify himself as the great explorer who had found his way through the uncharted wilderness of Antarctica but had lost his way in a Maine fog.

If the fog is thick elsewhere, it seems to be twice as thick and at least twice as frequent east of Schoodic.

"East of Schoodic" is familiar Maine nomenclature. The peninsula that juts out as the eastern boundary of Frenchman Bay is named Schoodic after an early Indian tribe. It divides the Maine coast into two parts as distinctively, for the sailor at least, as the Rockies divide the continent.

East of Schoodic the tides, like the fog, seem to run stronger, the waves are higher, the rockbound coast is even rockier, and the harbors of refuge are fewer and harder of entry. And inland the country is not so forested, not so green.

For all these reasons this area hasn't known the growth of summer colonies with anything like the profusion found west of Schoodic. The natives, mostly fishermen, are as rugged a race as you'll find in North America. Although they are fiercely independent, they are quick to extend a helping hand to the sailor in need, as the painter Ray Ellis found when he nearly went on the rocks at Moose Peak Light in a dense fog, and lobsterman David Look came upon him and led him to safety.

The first major port as one sails eastward from Schoodic is Jonesport, famous for its lobster boats, which are higher in the bow and narrower of beam than boats built elsewhere.

The Jonesport lobstermen equip them with the biggest automobile engines they can find, and they have an extraordinary turn of speed. When one comes at you, plunging through the whitecaps with a curtain of spray from that formidable bow, you think you are being run down by a destroyer.

Just beyond Jonesport is Roque Island, something of a geographical anomaly. This almost perfect crescent forms a well-protected bay, which can be a welcome haven in this area. But the salient feature is the beach.

On Maine's rocky coast, sand beaches are pocket-sized. They can be measured in feet, if not in inches. But Roque's beach is wide and the sand is soft, and it even seems that the water is warmer than elsewhere — that is, survivable by the hardy.

The harbors east of Roque are not without some charm and definitely are prominent in our history.

Our first naval engagement almost certainly came at Machias. When the news of the Battle of Lexington arrived in the busy little town, its four hundred or so souls erected a liberty pole and were promptly ordered to take it down by Captain Moore of HMS *Margaretta*, which happened to be in port.

The incensed people of Machias chased Moore back to his vessel and jeered his departure, working themselves up into such a lather of patriotic fervor that forty of them, a few with muskets but most with pitchforks, piled aboard the sloop *Unity* lying at the wharf and set sail in pursuit under the command of the fiery patriot Jeremiah O'Brien.

They were still within sight of shore when the faster *Unity* overtook the *Margaretta* and, despite the Britisher's fourteen swivel guns, let loose a broadside of musket fire. A lucky shot hit the *Margaretta*'s helmsman, the schooner broached, O'Brien ran his bowsprit through the Britisher's sail, and, with the boats thus locked together, the Americans swarmed aboard brandishing their pitchforks.

The experienced British sailors may have faced muskets and bayonets but not pitchforks. They panicked and surrendered the ship — a first for Machias and for a brand-new nation.

By the way, many of the nation's blueberries come from the barrens of Washington County behind Machias, the county seat.

Machias is more famous recently for a bitter battle waged over the dreams of some to establish in its deep water a port for super-tankers. Environmentalists successfully fought the plan, not the least of their concern being the fear of catastrophic spills that could endanger the precious bird sanctuary off Machias.

Along with Matinicus Rock, Machias's bird sanctuary has a thriving puffin population as well as a handsome gathering of those crossword-puzzle birds, auks, known more familiarly as razorbills. Standing upright and decked out in white shirts and black suits, they look amazingly like child-birds playing at being penguins.

Modern science has encroached on Cutler, thirteen miles on eastward. The hills above that lovely inlet are now marked by twenty-six huge towers spotted over a 2,800-acre site — the most powerful radio sending station in the world and the Navy's vital link with its submarines prowling the ocean deeps. What a far cry from the lighthouses that beamed their messages barely to the horizon!

Fifteen miles farther along, the United States comes to an end, not with the whispering gentleness of Key West at the other end of the eastern frontier but with the deafening crash of waves beating against the rocks below the candy-striped lighthouse at West Quoddy Head, the nation's easternmost point.

The nearest town is Lubec, once a prosperous sardine-canning center. It is the gateway to Campobello, the Canadian island where Franklin D. Roosevelt summered and where he contracted the polio that crippled him.

In his youth FDR was an avid sailor. Undoubtedly from a young lifetime of fighting the fierce tides that run through Cobscook Bay, he conjured up the dream that was to lead to one of his most vigorous congressional battles, one he was doomed to lose. That was his grandiose scheme to dam the Cobscook at Passamaquoddy and harness the eighteen-foot tides. He contended that enough electricity could be generated to power most of the East Coast.

Although the rising sun first touches the United States at the peak of Maine's over-five-thousand-foot-high Mount Katahdin, many, perhaps most, of the tourists who visit the Eastport, Lubec, and Quoddy Head region arrange to get up before dawn at least once in order to share its distinction of being the first populated area in the United States bathed in the new day's light.

"You people who live here must sort of take a pride in that," I suggested to an older resident watching with me as the tide surged around the bridge pilings at Lubec.

"Well," he said, "tell the truth, never thought much about it."

The Southeast

"THIS IS THE REAL AMERICA," Joe Cobb said. His right arm swept a wide arc, left to right, north to south. Joe was standing on a weather-beaten dock in Beaufort, North Carolina, his feet solidly planted on almost three hundred years of history.

Cobb pushed up the long-peaked cap shading a face tanned the color of expensive saddle leather, shading eyes with a permanent squint from scores of years of squeezing them against the glare of the southern sun.

The "real America" lies at various longitudes and latitudes across our broad land, depending on who defines it. The Middle West of the corn and wheat farmer is real America; so are the plains and hills of the Texas rancher, the apple orchards and potato fields of the Pacific north-westerner, and the teeming streets of the northeastern city dweller.

But to a Carolinian and sailmaker whose life was bound up with the water, the Intracoastal Waterway defined America, and he had a good case to make. For along the 1,245 miles that the Waterway snakes roughly south by southeast from Norfolk, Virginia, to Key West, Florida, there are samplings and slices and big chunks of all the countless elements and qualities that make up the endlessly surprising colossus that Joe Cobb called, simply, America.

On the banks of the Waterway there are elegant mansions on whose terraces the wealthy sip vintage wines with gourmet meals, and there are tumbledown shanties where the fisherman's fare depends on that day's catch. There are colleges with impressive reputations and island schoolhouses whose pupils commute by boat. There are, along the rivers, bays, and canals of this water highway, hamlets and cities, cottage industries and sprawling industrial complexes, one-house farms and vast plantations, rural bus stops and a rocket launching pad, country churches with steeples reaching for the sky and backwater coves where narcotics are smuggled ashore.

It's all here, Joe Cobb's real America, and if it sounds hopelessly heterogeneous, wait. . . . There is a common heritage on the Waterway; a soul, if you will. The same threads sew together life from Maryland to Florida.

The homogeneity of the Southeast Coast is woven of the water, and the boats, and the fish, and the birds, of a way of life and of history.

It all really starts and ends with the water. The people came in the beginning of our American civilization by water, they first expanded their tenuous foothold on a new continent by water, they held it against seaborne invasion, and they eked out from it the bare sustenance of survival.

We were founded in a manner of speaking on that coast, and it is almost allegorical that the first settlers who established the colony of Roanoke should have made it ashore through one of the most fickle bodies of water on the face of the globe.

Tug and barge on Intracoastal Waterway

We know it now as Cape Hatteras, and off that bleak point, ship-sinking, man-killing storms are bred with such suddenness as to defy even today's forecasters. These storms are born of a collision of elements as the Gulf Stream moves up from the south to meet the cool waters from the north sweeping out from the shore.

Early adventurers were lucky to make it in their tiny vessels across the Atlantic, luckier still in their last few miles to make it past Hatteras with its vile weather tantrums and its hidden shoals.

It was partly to beat those storms off Hatteras that the south-eastern peoples carved out one of the world's great waterways. Far earlier than road or railway, telegraph or telephone, boats linked the settlements of the coast — fast little cutters that brought the mail and the news, lumbering schooners and three-masters that carried the stuff of commerce. These vessels fought their way out and back through tricky inlets with their shifting shoals, clawed their way along stormy coasts, not infrequently in our past ran a gauntlet of raiders, legal and illegal, and left the shoreline dotted with the wreckage of ships and lives and hopes.

Long after sail had given way to steam and diesel, danger lurked on the outer coast. With the United States' entry into World War II, German U-boats sneaked to within sight of our southeastern shore. By April of 1942, coastal residents could see the explosions and fires of their night attacks; even in daylight billowing columns of smoke marked the death of another ship.

Twenty-three Allied vessels went down in these coastal waters in April alone. As much cargo as possible was shifted to barges and lighters to take the safe Waterway route, but this was too slow for the mounting traffic. Another way was found, and the slumbering ports suddenly were bustling with activity they'd never known before.

Key West, Jacksonville, Charleston, and Norfolk became the keys to what the Navy called its "bucket brigade." Convoys of Allied ships carrying oil and arms to Europe worked their way up the Atlantic coast in stages, sailing by day protected by corvettes and destroyers in jumps of 120 miles or so, and laying over at night in safe harbors while the warships turned around to go back for another trip.

The bucket brigade eventually reached all the way from the oil island of Aruba in the Dutch West Indies to Halifax, Nova Scotia, where the big transatlantic convoys formed up.

So, from colonial days to World War II, the work went on to link the bays and rivers by canals to provide the safe passage that is today known as the Intracoastal Waterway.

In recent years, up to fifteen thousand vessels annually make a substantial part of that trip. Not even the Army Corps of Engineers, which maintains the Waterway, can count the tens of thousands of other boats that, for recreation, fishing, or commerce, ply some narrower distance between the towns that cling to its wondrous edges.

Together, transits and locals are a passing panorama of every sort of vessel by which people today go to sea — from tiny, home-built rowboats that would look dangerous in a backyard swimming pool to the nuclear submarines and aircraft carriers that cross the Waterway to Savannah, Jacksonville, or Norfolk.

Sailors back from mysterious missions in distant waters hang on the rail and gaze down with wonder and amusement at those who find their recreation on a boat, even as the latter gaze up in awe at the mighty machines that could crush them to oblivion.

In the spring and fall the Waterway churns with the pleasure boats following the sun south or north, a parade of both opulence and dreams — the sixty-, seventy-, one-hundred-foot floating palaces whose paid captains are rushing them to impatient owners; the family-crewed sail-boats whose hailing ports bespeak colder climes; and occasionally the small sloop whose tattered ensign of another nation, rusty topsides, and self-steering vane whisper of the ocean adventurer's lonesome passage.

And all year 'round move the barges and their powerful tugs, huge carriers of commerce that to the smaller oncoming boat frequently seem to fill the narrower canals from bank to bank. Often the roaring turbines are called on to drive the blunt-faced barges through the silt that lines the shallow bottom, as they dig their own channels and help the engineers in a never-ending task of keeping the Waterway open.

The Intracoastal in the truest sense is not a canal, although it is that, too. For most of its distance it is a channel, dredged to ten or fifteen feet deep. The Waterway cuts down the center of bayous and creeks, and across bays, estuaries, and salt marshes that stretch miles wide behind the beaches of Georgia and the Carolinas. Finally, it connects the island-dotted, hip-deep expanse of water between Miami and Key West.

So serpentine is the route through the marshes that it is not unusual for a day's boat trip to cover only the straight-line distance that traffic on the shoreside highways leaps in half an hour.

There are long, straight stretches that truly are canals, dug out of the solid earth, their sides clean and smooth, their depths carried right to the banks. Most are of recent vintage, clawed out by modern mach-inery. But the oldest, at the northern end, was conceived and begun by George Washington and dug, laborious shovelful after shovelful, by hundreds of slaves.

Navigation down the Waterway is from pillar to post, along a route impeccably marked with signs planted in the water — red triangles on one side, green squares on the other, sometimes a few yards apart, occasionally separated by miles across the sounds. Woe awaits the sailor

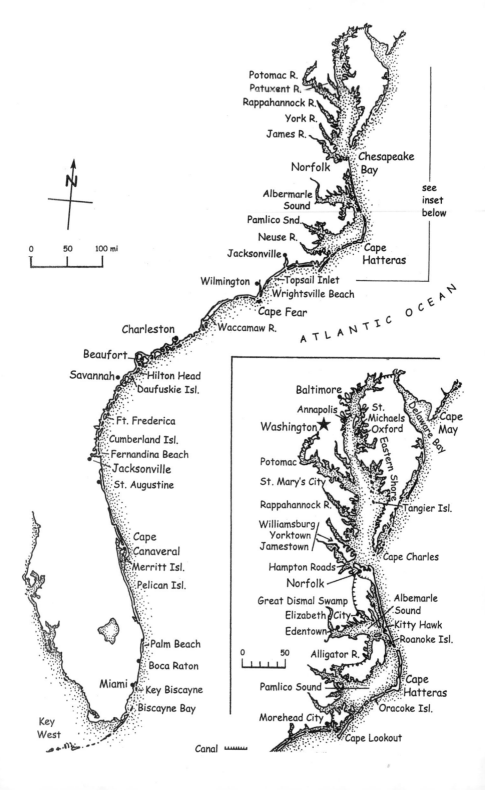

Potomac R.
Patuxent R.
Rappahannock R.
York R.
James R.

Norfolk

Chesapeake
Bay

Albermarle
Sound
Pamlico Snd.
Neuse R.

Jacksonville

Wilmington
Topsail Inlet
Wrightsville Beach
Cape Fear
Waccamaw R.

Cape
Hatteras

see
inset
below

N

0   50   100 mi

Charleston

Beaufort

Savannah
Hilton Head
Daufuskie Isl.

Ft. Frederica
Cumberland Isl.
Fernandina Beach
Jacksonville
St. Augustine

Cape
Canaveral
Merritt Isl.
Pelican Isl.

Palm Beach

Boca Raton

Miami
Key Biscayne

Biscayne Bay

Key
West

ATLANTIC OCEAN

Baltimore

Annapolis
St.
Michaels
Oxford

Washington ★

Delaware Bay

Cape
May

Eastern Shore

Potomac

St. Mary's City

Rappahannock R.

Tangier Isl.

Williamsburg
Yorktown
Jamestown

Cape Charles

Hampton Roads

Norfolk

Great Dismal Swamp
Elizabeth City
Edentown

Albemarle
Sound

Kitty Hawk
Roanoke Isl.

0   50

Alligator R.

Cape
Hatteras

Pamlico Sound

Oracoke Isl.

Morehead City

Cape Lookout

Canal 〰〰〰

whose attention strays.

The going can be tedious, but the rewards are unending. There are passages, notably in the Great Dismal Swamp of Virginia and along the lovely Waccamaw River in South Carolina, where the trees overhang the water, leaving an avenue of light only at the top as their branches almost join. One can navigate down the middle of those ways by staying under that ribbon of sunlight — or, for a somewhat riskier but unforgettable experience, by moonlight.

The marshes have a beauty of their own that only the boatman can experience. The tall saw grass that seems to wilt under the blazing noonday sun glories in the dawn. It reaches for the rising day, speckled by dew that catches the first light and, vaporizing, tinges the morning with a delicate mist.

The miracle of rebirth comes every day to the marshes as wildfowl stir to the day's endeavors. The long-legged cranes and egrets step their careful way through the shallow waters, and pelicans swoop in graceful flight above the water's surface, each seeking in its own way the sustenance those waters hold.

And humans are there, too, on the same search. Across the marshes, through the dawn's mist, move the shrimp and crab boats, only the tops of their superstructures above the grass showing their progress down the creeks to the open water.

The gulls and pelicans will follow them until each boat will have its own cloud of airborne freeloaders, the quarrelsome gulls squabbling over a choice morsel in the nets, the dignified pelicans lying back to dive-bomb the errant prey that will fill their cavernous beaks.

Moving out also in the early light are the sportfishermen and those whose daily catch will dictate that evening's menu for self and kin. Their game is the same, but their methods are as different as their inclinations and, more important, their means.

Out of the major population centers and the fancy resorts that now dot the Southeast Coast, the large boats roar, their owners racing to the fishing grounds offshore where they hope to find the big ones whose fight for life will provide a day's recreation.

Along the endless beaches, fancy new four-wheel vehicles and converted jalopies, with outsized tires to support them in the sinking sand, meet the morning at the surf's edge. They'll be relieved of the long poles that stand on front bumpers and the hip-high boots in back, and their occupants will cast for the fish that dare lurk so close to the human domain.

Along the Waterway others will trudge with fishing pole over their shoulders, a bucket of bait in one hand and perhaps a cooler of beer in the other, to take up their stations on piers or abandoned bridges that permit them.

And all along the water, concrete ramps mark the modern marriage of automobile and boat. Just before dawn come the cars and trailers, their lights winking their way to the water's edge. Here the universal fraternity of fishermen perhaps is at its most democratic.

Shiny new Mercedes or rusty old Chevy; sleek fiberglass with four hundred horses inboard or hand-hewn pine with ten horses hung on the transom; sport shirt from Brooks Brothers or blue denim from Penney's — here at the ramp, theirs is a classless society. Sports Shirt is there wrestling Blue Denim's boat off the trailer, and the favor is returned in kind.

Some of these may be "locals," although probably not. The natives keep their boats hauled up in their own yards. Trailered boats have come from a greater distance — inland, from exclusive retirement communities, or from working-class districts that service the industries that have been flooding south this last half century.

First the railroad, then the highway, and now the airport have altered the character of the Southeast, as, of course, they have changed every accessible spot on Earth. The change was gradual at first, and then it accelerated drastically after World War II. There is still open beach stretching mile after mile down the Atlantic Coast, and there are belated government and private efforts to preserve it and its irreplaceable wildlife for future generations.

From Norfolk to Cape Hatteras, the dunes have almost disappeared under the shoulder-to-shoulder beach houses. The barrier islands off South Carolina and Georgia offer resort living in country club surroundings; it has become a permanent way of life for an increasing number of well-to-do retirees.

The epitome, of course, is Florida. Wild palmetto palms, which grace the shore from Savannah south, give way to a transplanted variety, carefully placed to landscape mansions and high-rise condominiums that line the Waterway in unending procession.

Against this tide in the still surprisingly large undeveloped sections, life goes on much as it has for a dozen generations.

Along these lonelier stretches of beach rise occasional houses perched precariously on stilts. The solitude-seeking owners hope they will protect them from the rising waters of a winter storm.

Until just a few years ago, one of the most interesting unspoiled pockets was Daufuskie Island in South Carolina. Except for the glow of lights from the neighboring resort island of Hilton Head and from Savannah a few miles to the south, one seemed to have arrived there by time machine, traveling back into another century.

Up from the dock, sandy lanes lead under moss-laden trees past kerosene-lighted cabins, an old frame church, and an eighteenth-century cemetery. The small stone crypt here was raided in the distant past, but through a hole punched in its side and with the help of a flashlight, one can see a now empty sarcophagus, its history and onetime occupant lost in time.

The natives mostly are black. From generations of isolation, most of them still speak with a lilting accent that is their own. There had always been a white presence, from the time the first plantation owner brought the blacks here, but never more than a few families, until a big resort squatted on one side of the island a few years ago.

Bud Bates ran the general store, and Oscar Snyder was the island's self-appointed engineer, if one was ever needed. He retired a couple of decades ago after glory years at sea, the last as chief engineer of the yacht of the late Rafael Trujillo, the Dominican Republic's onetime playboy dictator.

Oscar made up for the shy reticence of his fellow Daufuskians, and he was an effective spokesman.

"We don't need nothin' here 'cept what we got. I get my lunch and dinner sittin' right down there on the point. Get me a deer or possum or rabbit with my .22, and I put a pole right over there and get me some of the best trout you ever seen.

"Now some day I'm goin' to get me one of them Fippe boats like Mr. Fippe used to build — thirty feet long and as broad as she was long. A little sloop with a centerboard.

"The folks here used to take 'em down to Savannah to sell their potatoes and vegetables and hogs and stuff. Never heard of 'em losin' a man. Yep, if I live long enough, I'm goin' to build me one of them.

"I been to New York and San Francisco and all those seaports, and I ain't seen no reason to be anywhere but here. 'Course it ain't goin' to stay like this. Those developers are sniffin' around."

They were sniffing, indeed, and even before their development, one by one, more modern homes were encroaching on Daufuskie's unique solitude.

Some winters ago they tore down the blue-fronted, one-room Soul Club. A newcomer wanted the lumber for his recreation room.

Although not as remote, but just as isolated from the mainstream of modern life, are the small fishing settlements that speckle the Waterway. The fishermen's cabins, as weathered and careworn as their inhabitants, cling with uncertainty to their toehold on the bank. Tethered below are their boats. In South Carolina and Georgia they are often home-built bateaux.

From those small, shallow-draft, blunt-ended scows, they fish as their great-grandfathers did — minding crab pots or tonging oysters with ten-foot-long "pliers," a few at a time from dawn until dusk, until they have all they can carry or all that a supply diminished by overfishing and modern pollution will provide.

They share this problem with their wealthier brothers, the commercial shrimpers, crabbers, and oystermen. The resorts and marinas serving the sportfishermen and the transient yachts are an increasingly important part of the Southeast Coast's economy, but the mainstay industry still is the commercial fishery. Even that is beginning to languish as the boats must go farther afield, and their own waters are fished by more and more foreigners. A foreigner is a foreigner here, whether he comes from Florida or from Russia.

Of all the boats fishing for profit along our coasts, none are so glorious as the Chesapeake Bay's skipjacks, an anachronism dictated by law. Maryland, in a farsighted and ingenious move to protect its oyster beds from rampant exploitation, years ago limited the fishing of them to boats *under sail.* That has been relaxed now to permit other, more modern methods, and the skipjacks sadly are disappearing.

At the turn of the century, there were hundreds of them plying the Bay. Today their number has dwindled to barely ten. The oldest still working the beds is the *Ruby G. Ford,* whose keel was laid in 1895. The newest was Ashford's *Anna McGarvey,* built in 1981.

Properly, they are called two-sail bateaux, but by modern nomenclature they are sloops — a single mast raked at a jaunty angle with a boom so long it overhangs the transom of these forty- to sixty-foot beauties. A pleasant sheer gives them a racy look but, more practically, lowers the deck midships to ease the hauling of the dredge and its payload.

A graceful bowsprit carries the big foresail, and amidships a low house provides room for a stove and a toilet, while at the stern a taffrail finishes off a design that is eminently practical. But, in the manner of such pragmatism, it turns out to be delightfully aesthetic as well.

They are manned by a captain and four crewmen — in good

Chesapeake Bay, Skipjacks

times, of which there haven't been many lately, a cook is added. Most of them are natives of Tilghman Island or nearby Deal — second-, third-, and fourth-generation inheritors of a tradition, but there are newcomers too, lured by the romance of that tradition. A graduate of an exclusive northeastern boarding school counted among them for several years. He learned to call things by their right name: They "drudge" for oysters; the bowsprit is the "bowsplit"; and the small yawl boats that provide the skipjacks' only source of power hang off the stern from "davids," never davits.

Lost with the diminishing skipjack fleet was one of the grandest regattas to be seen anywhere. The annual skipjack race offshore, near Annapolis, brought visitors from far and wide. Loaded aboard each boat were all the relatives and friends the deck could hold. The competition was fierce, and the honor of winning was prized almost as much as the catch the boats would glean over a hard winter's work. Today the remaining boats still race, now off Tilghman Island, in a far more informal event.

The skipjack fleet is but one of the unique features that makes the Chesapeake what it is — the grand foyer for any trip south by southeast down America's Atlantic Coast. For here, also, begins that chain of towns and villages and cities around which our history has developed.

It starts at Baltimore, at the northwestern head of the Chesapeake — the Baltimore that gave us, among other things, the "Star-Spangled Banner."

In the sticky, hot August of 1814, British troops had advanced on Washington and burned the Capitol and the White House, but they needed the port of Baltimore to sustain their forces ashore.

The Maryland militia turned the Redcoats back at the approaches to the city, and Fort McHenry denied them access from the water.

The British fleet lay just out of range of the fort, and one day in September a Baltimore lawyer rowed out to its flagship, the HMS *Surprise*, to try to effect the release of a prisoner. He had the poor luck to get there just as HMS *Surprise* and her fleet were moving in to attack Fort McHenry.

As an unwilling spectator, the lawyer watched for thirty hours as the British unceasingly bombarded the fort. On the dawn of the second day, he saw the tattered fifteen-stripe flag of the young Republic still flying over the ramparts and was moved to scribble a poem. Later, Francis Scott Key's words were set to the tune of, ironically, an old British tavern song, and the national anthem was born.

Baltimore's place in our naval and maritime history is secure, and continues. Today, as one of the nation's largest cities, it is a port of call for ships of more than ninety lines from all over the world. And in its rebuilt and revitalized inner harbor is permanently moored that hoary veteran of the sea wars and oldest naval ship afloat, the USS *Constellation*.

Baltimore gave not only an anthem to our history but also one of the sleekest and swiftest sailing vessels ever to split the waves. The *Baltimore Clipper*, for her speed and maneuverability, became a favorite of armed privateers that slipped down Chesapeake Bay to take their toll of British shipping during the War of 1812.

The Eastern Shore that stretches below Baltimore is not just a geographical designation of the vast peninsula that encloses Chesapeake Bay on the east. It names also a way of life that for almost 130 years was an island cut off from the megalopolis growing along the mainland.

The Eastern Shore's natural link to the mainland was severed in 1829, when the government completed an old plan of Benjamin Franklin's and cut a canal between the Chesapeake and the Delaware bays at their northern end. Narrow bridges spanned the canal, but the

Eastern Shore was left to slumber. It preserved a gentle culture more similar to the English countryside than to the brawling, bustling mainland America busily pushing out its frontiers and building its cities.

Gentlemen farmers built great mansions and spent their days riding to hounds or hunting in their duck blinds, while their servants tended the crops and fished the streams.

In 1952, engineers spanned the Chesapeake across its five-mile narrows just above Annapolis, and the burgeoning populations of Washington-Baltimore spewed onto the Eastern Shore. The once pristine Atlantic beach is now dotted with high-rise hotels and condominiums. High taxes, expensive help, and lucrative bids from developers have begun breaking up some of the old estates.

Still, a surprising number of the old plantations, the old mansions, and the old ways persist. Houses stand resplendent under spreading oak and elm, magnolia and juniper trees at the tops of lawns that sweep down to the docks at the creek's edge. Stables still house fine horses, and the lovely Labrador and Chesapeake retrievers eagerly await their master's call for an early morning hunt.

The towns that lie up the rivers and creeks of the Eastern Shore are as pretty as any you'll ever find, St. Michaels and Oxford the gems among them. With Annapolis a half-day's sail on the opposite shore, they form a triangle of boating activity so intense that carefree sailing frequently must give way to careful attention to the rules of the road, particularly in the spring and fall. These are the favorite months. In spring, the shores are reborn green and briefly white with dogwood blossoms. The southerly winds are soft as kisses, and the cool night breezes find their way up under the trees to touch the most remote anchorage.

Autumn brings the pageant of the changing, flaming foliage on the banks of the bay. Temperatures are still comfortable and storms infrequent.

Although both are blessed with their good days, winter and summer tend to be extreme on Chesapeake Bay. In July and August temperatures soar high into the nineties, and sudden thunderstorms, black and savage, are frequent. As for winter, well, the Chesapeake isn't quite far enough south.

Annapolis today is one of the world's great yachting centers. Once quiet Spa and Back Creeks that bound it on the south now are lined with tasteful low-rise condominiums. Their waters are parking lots for hundreds of sailboats, as are the creeks that feed the beautiful Severn River to the north.

Racing fleets are so numerous that on busy weekends their courses trace an intricate, interlocking pattern across the bay. Cruising boats make for a dozen destinations, such as St. Michaels, whose tiny natural harbor fills early for a floating cocktail party.

They all sail in the shadow of history. Annapolis was the capital of the sprouting United States in 1783 and 1784, when the peripatetic Continental Congress sat there for six months. The handsome state house, which hosted the Congress, has the distinction of being the oldest state capitol in continuous use. George Washington resigned here as commander in chief of the Continental Army, and the Continental Congress ratified the 1784 Treaty of Paris, ending the Revolutionary War.

The harbor comes right up to the center of Annapolis, and the waterfront has undergone a good deal of rebuilding and restoration, preserving its colonial charm. The street lamps in City Dock Park are replicas of the oil lamps that burned there more than two hundred years ago.

It is a fortunate visitor who finds himself in Annapolis on May Day. Tiny brick houses work their way up narrow streets to the state house; on their front doors baskets of spring flowers greet the arrival of another vernal season. Commercial and public buildings join the ceremony, and a flower basket always graces the guardhouse at Gate One of the Naval Academy. The academy, of course, is a pervasive presence in Annapolis. The grounds extend from the town center back to the Severn. Middies throng the city streets, and never more so than in June Week, with its round of parades, ceremonies, and celebrations for the newly commissioned ensigns.

Little St. Michaels has been touched by history, too. During the War of 1812, according to local legend, the good people of St. Michaels hung lanterns in treetops behind the town to fool the cannoneers of British warships offshore. As a result, the British gunners overshot St. Michaels, and most of their cannonballs fell harmlessly among the trees. Most, but not quite all. One cannonball went through the roof of a house on the edge of town, rolled down the stairway and through the front door to come to rest on the lawn. The building today is known, logically enough, as Cannonball House.

Legends also speak of pirates at lovely Oxford, lying quietly at the mouth of the Tred Avon. The pleasant Robert Morris Inn, opened in 1710, leads a parade of handsome colonial houses up its broad main street.

Story has it that the notorious "Blackbeard" paid an Oxford boat-builder with a sackful of gold coins, so many of them that they covered a tabletop. Boat owners of today won't find the story unlikely.

Oxford was a major port in the seventeenth and eighteenth centuries. From its docks, as from those of its twin town of Cambridge up the neighboring Choptank River (of course, Cambridge — where there's an Oxford there must be a Cambridge), sailed the vessels carrying to England the baled leaves from the tobacco plantations that first brought this area its riches.

Some of the great porticoed plantation homes still stand, notably one rather grandly called My Lady Sewell's Manor. It dates back to the 1660s and is one of the oldest on the Eastern Shore.

History, of course, didn't skip the Western Shore, the very names bespeaking the past when the waterways were the principal avenues of commerce. Up South River, just down a bit from Annapolis, are Warehouse, Church, and Brewer Creeks, and Almshouse Creek, where the old county poorhouse still stands.

Antipoison Creek acquired that wonderfully descriptive name because Captain John Smith, wounded by a stingray, was treated successfully with a poultice of mud from the creek — an old Indian remedy.

Not so clear, however, is how other names were acquired. An island in Solomon's Harbor off the Patuxent River is called Molly's Leg, in fond memory, perhaps. And one wonders whether there is any associative connection between Molly's Leg and Cuckold Creek, a little distance away.

The Patuxent River harbors our past and our future. At its mouth is the sprawling Naval Air Station, which breeds astronauts and test pilots with "the right stuff." And farther up its reaches is a working link to yesteryear, Sotterley, a spacious estate with a house dating to 1717.

Sotterley is a picture-book plantation with lawns running to the river's edge, and an old "rolling road" down which hogsheads of meat and tobacco were rolled to the river docks where ships waited to carry them across the seas. Flocks of sheep graze on Sotterley's leas, and in the smokehouse huge hams hang to be cured as they were one hundred years ago. It's all for real; Sotterley is a working plantation still.

It was up the Patuxent that the British vessels sailed in August

1814 in order to land their troops at Benedict, eighteen miles inland. The troops marched from there on Washington. The fleet's passage was not unobstructed, however, and in the Calvert Marine Museum are artifacts recovered from gun barges sunk in the Patuxent in a game effort to stop the English ships.

Barely a morning's sail down the Chesapeake is the Potomac, the river that the ever-foresighted John Smith named from an Indian word meaning "Where tribute is brought." How in the world did Captain Smith know that the city of Washington would be settled on the banks of that river?

It is the unlucky sailor who arrives off the Potomac when river current and tide are running against each other, and together are being whipped by a strong northwest wind coming down the river valley. It can make the waters between Point Lookout on the north and Smith Point on the south as ornery as any the bay will see. But the long, lazy trip up the Potomac is worth a little discomfort.

On its banks is one of our historical treasures, George Washington's magnificent Mount Vernon. Farther downstream, and up the tributary that is the St. Marys River, Leonard Calvert sailed the *Ark* and the *Dove* to establish Maryland's first settlement. At St. Marys City, Maryland's first state house was built in 1676. The reconstructed building now stands on a high hill overlooking the river.

Later history is reflected up Cockrell Creek where impressive Victorian homes in Reedville attest to the prosperity of the menhaden fisheries, which still are the town's major industry (and the source of a barely endurable stench when the wind is wrong).

The Rappahannock, three miles wide at its mouth, once was a major avenue of commerce. Fredericksburg, ninety-three miles upriver, was a major port until choked off by a Union blockade in the Civil War. With its eighteenth-century houses and other colonial buildings, it remains a tourist's delight, although river traffic today is limited to a few barges.

At Ferry Farm, George Washington threw *whatever* it was across the Rappahannock. Legend says it was a silver dollar; revisionists claim it was a stone — if anything. At any rate, he did attend school at Ferry Farm.

Back across the bay, sea-broad there, lie the fascinating islands of Smith and Tangier, barely brought by high-speed powerboats and television into the twentieth century. Their people are fishermen whose roots dig two centuries into the sandy soil.

The islands much resemble each other — white frame houses behind weather-grayed piers, waiting forever for the painters who will never come. At every pier there is a boat for crabbing, the main business of the islands. In winter they "drudge" the bottom for blue crabs, and in summer baited pots are dropped to lure them.

Dove

On Smith a "main street" of water runs through the biggest town of Ewell. Tangier, too, is cut by a canal that splits the island. Tylerton's grammar school children take the boat across main street to school in Ewell, and high schoolers commute daily to the mainland — a trip on fair days more romantic than the yellow school bus, but one that's stripped of pleasure in winter when freezing northers roil Tangier Sound.

It was on Tangier that the British made their headquarters in the War of 1812. Descendants of those who put up with the occupation scarcely ever remark on the fact, as though it were a matter of personal shame. This is a rare manifestation of historical reticence in our southeastern states, where the most insignificant incident deserves a plaque, and the more significant occurrences have given rise to entire villages of cottage industry in maps, tours, costumes, and souvenirs.

One boatman, who finally has found a snug harbor at Marathon in the Florida Keys, has commemorated the impression that all these tourist exhibits have made on him. He has written in cement supporting an old naval gun his sardonic tribute:

This is a concrete example of an
AUTHENTIC REPRODUCTION
of a
GENUINE REPLICA
of an
ANTIQUE CANNON
Similar to those on board
ANCIENT SPANISH GALLEONS.

And he has noted that this is "Hysterical Marker No. 1."

Our genuine history began in many ways at the lower end of the Chesapeake, where the James and York rivers part to cradle the Virginia peninsula.

The British epoch on these shores began and ended there, just a few miles apart.

The first permanent English settlement in America was established at Jamestown in mid-May 1607 — May 13 or 14, history hasn't made up its mind. And on the other side of the peninsula at Yorktown, British General Cornwallis surrendered 174 years later, effectively bringing an end to the Revolutionary War.

The capital of Virginia remained at Jamestown until 1699, when the seat of government was moved five miles inland to what was then Middle Plantation, to be renamed Williamsburg. Today it is surely the finest of all colonial restorations.

The first Anglican church in the New World was built at Jamestown in 1639, and its tower still stands. It was on Chickahominy Creek, just four miles above Jamestown, that the Indian maiden Pocahontas, daughter of mighty chief Powhatan, threw herself over Captain John Smith to save the intrepid explorer from her revengeful tribespeople. Her place in history was further assured when she married colonist John Rolfe and produced one of America's first families.

The yachtsman about to enter the Intracoastal Waterway at Norfolk sails through Hampton Roads in a regatta of ghost ships whose names are written large in our naval history.

Norfolk itself suffered one of the most intensive naval bombardments of the Revolutionary War. Its ruin came on New Year's Day, 1777, after the town gallantly refused a British ultimatum to feed the hungry crews of its fleet lying just off the docks. "Feed us or we'll fire" was Lord Dunmore's demand. Norfolk didn't, and the British fleet did.

Eighty-eight guns of five warships leveled the thriving town of six thousand souls in just three hours, and drunken, looting colonial troops completed the destruction.

Norfolk is still rebuilding its waterfront, although now it is removing the ravages of time and not the dirty work of the Royal Navy. Today it is one of the dramatically resurgent cities of the Southeast Coast.

The ironclad Confederate warship *Merrimac* was built up the nearby Elizabeth River to do battle with the ironclad Union *Monitor* in the most memorable naval engagement of the Civil War. And from Newport News across the way have come the mighty aircraft carriers *Forrestal* and *Enterprise*, as well as the onetime queens of transatlantic liners — *America* and the *United States*.

(On the captain's desk of the *Enterprise*, the largest war vessel ever launched, there is a little plaque much favored by the skippers of far smaller boats. It is the seaman's prayer: "O Lord, protect me, for my boat is so small and your ocean is so large.")

Sailing past the Portsmouth and Norfolk navy yards, one is under the shadows of American naval might for the better part of an hour — aircraft carriers, cruisers, destroyers, supply and hospital ships, and nuclear submarines, menacing even at rest.

There are more broad waters to cross on our cruise south by southeast — the great sounds, Albemarle and Pamlico — but now the greatest, the Chesapeake, is behind us, and at Norfolk the canals of the Waterway proper begin.

Immediately a decision must be made — whether to take the Virginia Cut or the Dismal Swamp route south. The Virginia Cut has its merits: it is well marked and offers fairly smooth sailing. But the Dismal Swamp Canal is more fun — and it has a couple of ghosts to offer for added spice.

The Great Dismal Swamp itself begins in Virginia and extends into North Carolina, covering 350 square miles. Its first surveyor, Colonel William Byrd II, who looked it over in 1728, found it to be a "vast body of dirt and nastiness." Whereas Byrd saw the bottle half empty, George Washington, surveying the swamp only thirty-five years later, found the bottle half full. He called the swamp "a glorious paradise."

It could not have been all bad. The Irish poet Thomas Moore sat by the side of Lake Drummond in the middle of the swamp one evening in 1803 and was inspired to write a poem based on a local Indian legend. The story was about a young brave whose sweetheart had died. In his grief, he believed she had risen from her grave and gone into the swamp. He followed her there, himself to die and be with his beloved. As Moore wrote, the Indian lovers

Dismal Swamp Canal

Are seen at the hour of midnight damp

To cross the lake by a fire-fly lamp,

And paddle their white canoe.

In addition to Indian ghosts, bears are supposedly in the Great Dismal Swamp. Both are seen with about equal frequency.

Modern environmentalists may give the Father of our Country a bad mark, but the engineer in George Washington saw development possibilities in much that he surveyed. He became involved in a project to drain part of the swamp, that "glorious paradise," so its timber could be cut, and it was Washington who foresaw the canal through its eastern edge.

Thick stands of maples, oaks, pines, and poplars line the banks of the Dismal Swamp Canal, spreading their branches into a canopy overhead, as bald cypresses, eerie in the shadows, stand guard along the water's edge. In many places remnants can be seen of the timber wall built by slaves to keep the forest out of George Washington's canal. The weathering of the decades has worn the tops of the wall to ragged teeth barely breaking the water's surface, but these stand as testament to mankind's conquest of nature.

The canal today is not without its modern touches. A highway occasionally blights the view to one side, and on a recent passage my sailboat, *Wyntje*, bounced on a hard spot on the shallow bottom. "Somebody must've dumped another old automobile down there," the lockkeeper suggested. "Sometimes these fellows just strip a car and push it over the side of the canal. Good way to get rid of them."

Everywhere but here and on the neighboring Virginia Cut, the Waterway is a sea-level route. A twelve-foot difference between the Chesapeake and the Albemarle is compensated for on the Virginia Cut by one great machine-driven lock; two small locks operate on the Dismal

Swamp Canal, their gates ground shut by friendly keepers more than pleased to break monotonous routines by trading gossip with passing boatmen. The canal empties into the Pasquotank River, which takes its time winding thirty miles down to Elizabeth City, North Carolina, on an inlet of Albemarle Sound.

Around the corner on another inlet of Albemarle Sound is one of the handsomest of all of America's colonial villages, Edenton. Perhaps Edenton's beauty lies in its unpretentiousness. Its impeccably preserved eighteenth-century mansions sit serenely on manicured lawns undaunted by time, some of them silently saluting their neighbors across the town green.

In one home is an impressive display of Revolutionary crockery glued back together from pieces found buried deep in the backyard, where once the privy stood. Kitchen slaves sought to avoid punishment by dumping broken crockery there. A missing plate was more likely to escape detection than a broken one. For similar reasons archaeologists have long treasured such locations in researching other civilizations.

"Time Warp Syndrome" has been known to overcome a visitor stumbling on Edenton at its annual celebration of a local tea party that antedates even Boston's famous demonstration. The ladies of Edenton declared their own boycott of British tea to protest the tax upon it, and the town remembers this early display of feminine militancy with a costumed fair on the green. A mock battle is re-created between handsomely uniformed and drilled Yankees and Redcoats.

To the east a great sand spit forms the outer barrier beach that encloses Albemarle Sound, running from Norfolk past Cape Hatteras to Cape Lookout. Here at the Outer Banks begins that great chain of barrier islands that hug the Atlantic Coast of the Carolinas, Georgia, and Florida, their sanded contours constantly changing under the relentless assault of ocean storms.

Pirates once made their lair under the protection of these islands. Tucked behind Cape Hatteras around Ocracoke and Roanoke islands, the skull and crossbones flew with impunity.

The infamous Blackbeard met his end here, run aground by the Royal Navy sloop *Ranger* and boarded by Lieutenant Robert Maynard and his men. Maynard bested the pirate with pistols and sabers, inflicting, it is said, twenty-five wounds before Blackbeard toppled.

So impressed was Maynard with his victim's appearance — Blackbeard did up his long full beard in braids and tied the queues to his hair with multicolored ribbons — that he severed the head and sailed back to port with it mounted on the bowsprit.

Edward Teach, for such was Blackbeard's name, is still remembered around Ocracoke. Hundreds of boats run "Teach's Hole Channel" to reach one of the East Coast's most exciting fishing grounds.

Just up the beach from Ocracoke at a place called Kitty Hawk, the course of history was forever altered on a cool December day in 1903, when the Wright brothers first succeeded in powered flight.

Sixty-six years later, just behind the Waterway at Cape Canaveral in Florida, men would take off for the first exploration of the moon. It is noteworthy that both trips began on the water: the larger parts of the Apollo spacecraft arrived at the cape by barge; the Wright brothers sailed the pieces of their fragile craft to Kitty Hawk.

The Outer Banks were perfect for the Wrights — flat except for the gentle rise of Kill Devil Hill, with autumn winds blowing gently from the north and northeast. What attracted the daring Ohio bicycle builders now draws thousands of vacationers. The highway that traverses the beach is lined with houses perched on stilts by hopeful owners. A few houses are ravaged almost every year by the wind and waves and the constantly shifting beach line.

One of the nation's most famous lighthouses is candy-striped Hatteras Light, whose signal has blinked a warning of the treacherous coast to mariners since 1870. The great lighthouse, one of the world's tallest at 208 feet, as it entered the 1990s teetered on the edge of disaster. The sands that had protected it from the Atlantic had slowly eroded away. But at what worried engineers felt was the last minute, Congress appropriated twelve million dollars for the rescue endeavor.

A Buffalo, New York, engineering firm that had previously moved three much smaller lighthouses, the International Chimney Corporation, did the job. It inserted a bed of steel beams in the base of the 2,800-ton brick tower, and with hydraulic rams moved it along steel rails, five feet per push, half a mile down the beach to a safer home, 1,600 feet from the shore.

It would have been the ultimate irony if Hatteras Light had joined the more than two thousand vessels its valiant efforts have failed to guide to safety, and whose hulks now lie buried beneath the waves offshore.

The Hatteras storms arise without warning, sudden and violent. Driving rain and scud as white as snow whip from the tops of the breaking waves, blinding the mariner. The gales and the angry waves capsize smaller boats and wash larger ones onto shoals that extend far out to sea.

The experience can drive strong men insane. In one big storm, two yachtsmen who had taken to a life raft from their sinking sailboat abandoned its comparative security and their companions. As they dived into the shark-filled waters, one said calmly that he was going to the 7-Eleven for cigarettes.

Roanoke Island nestles under the lee of the Outer Banks, still obstinately refusing to give up the secret of its famous Lost Colony. Souvenir stands and Elizabethan taverns tell one proudly that here, four hundred years ago, occurred the first English attempt to settle the New World, and here was christened Virginia Dare, the first English child born into that world.

No one knows to this day what happened to the fifteen settlers left behind in 1586, when Sir Richard Grenville sailed back to England for reinforcements.

If the weather is kicking up outside and the winds are right, Albemarle Sound can be almost as nasty as the ocean. But across its broad reach there is the security of more sheltered waters — the Alligator River, the Pungo River Canal, and the Pamlico River, where much of North Carolina's pre-Revolutionary history was made.

Here, indeed, is the oldest town in the state — Bath, which before the Revolution was the capital of the province. To sail up to Bath is to follow another of Blackbeard's favorite routes. No one can be sure he ever sounded the *Queen Anne's Revenge* up to an anchorage here, but it

Cape Hatteras Lighthouse

is known that he came by smaller boat to enjoy rest and relaxation in congenial surroundings.

Local scandal has it that immunity from the law was bestowed on Teach through his friendship with Governor Charles Eden and through Tobias Knight, the secretary and collector of North Carolina and a judge on the Vice Admiralty Court. Eden (who gave his name to Edenton) even presided at Teach's ninth wedding — to a sixteen-year-old local girl.

This was during a brief period when Teach enjoyed a pardon, granted under an amnesty program intended to try to bring piracy under control. Teach appeared in Bath Town in the company of Stede Bonnet, as unlikely a pair of brigands as ever swaggered down the old capital's dusty streets.

Teach, a hulking rough-hewn sailor from Bristol, and Bonnet, an army major who fled a nagging wife on Barbados and bought a ten-gun ship to go a-pirating, decided to seek amnesty together. While in Bath enjoying himself, Bonnet learned that war had broken out between England and Spain. He secured privateer papers and returned to Topsail Inlet off Wilmington to rejoin his ship. He found, however, that Teach had gotten there ahead of him, stolen his boat, marooned his crew, and sailed for Ocracoke.

One of Bath's old school bells is said to have come from one of Blackbeard's ships; and when the northwest wind pushes the tide even farther out, the remains of what may have been a pirate ship peek from the river mud.

On the Neuse River, at the southwestern end of Pamlico Sound, lies a reminder that it wasn't just the British and, farther south, the Spanish who settled our southeastern states. New Bern was named by its Swiss and German colonists for Switzerland's largest canton. Not that the British influence is absent in New Bern. Its old Presbyterian church was built from plans drawn by London's renowned architect Sir Christopher Wren. And Tryon Palace, completed in 1767 as the seat of the royal provincial government, has been restored to its original elegance with formal gardens and priceless furnishings.

The Neuse River in foul weather can be as mean as Albemarle and Pamlico sounds, but then the Waterway winds down quiet Adams Creek to the Atlantic's first important port of entry below Norfolk. The twin cities of Morehead City and Beaufort make up a major shipping, fishing, and recreational boating center. They also represent a landfall and a jumping-off place for transatlantic sailors and those bound for the Bahamas or the Caribbean.

Tall ships lie at Beaufort's handsomely restored dock to resupply for their ocean passages. This third-oldest town in North Carolina, founded in 1709, has carefully restored much of its colonial heritage. Its ambitious Maritime Museum preserves through an apprentice program the Southeast Coast's famed boat-building skills. With loving devotion to a nearly lost craft, these artisans are turning out impressive replicas of the dories, dinghies, Whitehalls, and sharpies that once graced the local waters.

At the twin cities, at Wrightsville Beach farther south, and at countless other points along the Waterway, the inheritors of the boating industry thrive. Uncounted thousands have been employed since World War II, servicing the needs of the floating population. They include beribboned clerks in boutiques peddling doodads to satisfy the whims of the yachtsmen, and hard-hatted workers in modern factories breaking dozens of boats a day from their fiberglass molds.

Some are descendants of men who pounded together the great wooden fishing fleets, but most are immigrants lured by work in a climate more benign than that of their northeastern homelands. This is typical of the migration that is forever changing the social, economic, and political environment of the southeastern states.

Attractive Wrightsville Beach is representative of the new communities that have sprung up around boating centers. Drawing its principal sustenance from nearby Wilmington, it is a thriving town of its own now. High-rise condominiums and luxury homes border its broad beaches.

The development spreads north until it reaches Topsail Inlet, where apartments and stilted homes block the vista that once was Blackbeard's and Bonnet's as they took refuge in the tall saw grass of the marshes. Their pirate ships nestled there hidden from the oceanside, except when they hoisted their topsails to catch the wind and sally forth.

Just south of Wrightsville at the mouth of the Cape Fear River, which runs up to Wilmington, Bonnet met his end. Colonel William Rhett, in two armed sloops outfitted at his own expense, mounting a total of sixteen guns and 130 men, ran Bonnet aground. Rhett's boats were also aground, but Bonnet was within range. After five hours of pounding, the pirate surrendered, to be hanged at White Point, Charleston, six weeks later, on November 12, 1718.

Whatever Bonnet thought of Rhett's cannonade, it was as nothing compared with another on the Cape Fear River a century and a half later.

Toward the end of the Civil War, Wilmington was the last port open to Confederate blockade runners. Just who did the counting, and how, is not known, but local historians say that Confederate and British ships made 2,054 attempts to run the blockade up the river and that 1,735 of those ships got through — a success rate of 84 percent.

The ships were protected by two forts at the river's entrance — Forts Fisher and Anderson. In January 1865 a mighty Union armada of sixty ships and 6,000 troops appeared off Wilmington. They were under orders to seal off this final lifeline to the crumbling South.

The naval bombardment was the most intensive in history up until then, and wasn't to be matched until the Battle of Jutland in World War I. Fort Fisher fell quickly, but Fort Anderson held out for more than a month before it was overrun, and the Confederacy's fate was foretold.

The Cape Fear River claims another chapter in our history. Unlike England's Lost Colony, this event is largely forgotten. There is no pageant of the tragedy to rival Roanoke Island's popular drama of *The Lost Colony*.

In 1526, sixty years before that small band of English adventurers landed at Roanoke, five hundred Spanish from Santo Domingo under Lucas Velásquez de Ayloon settled at the mouth of a river they called the Río Jordan. It was almost certainly the Cape Fear. Apparently, the colony prospered for some years and then vanished. Its fate is unrecorded — and largely unremembered.

South of Wilmington, the Waterway hugs the land side of the South Brunswick Islands, a string of magnificent beaches that slope so gently into the ocean there is virtually no undertow. The Gulf Stream, now just fifty miles offshore, warms the water. Some of the three-story-high sand dunes pile up even to the Waterway's edge, reaching for the passing boatman.

Just as suddenly as a breaking wave and as if South Carolina had determined on a different decor, the landscape changes. Scarcely across the state line at Enterprise Landing, the Waterway enters one of its most beautiful reaches.

This is the Waccamaw River and its tributary Prince Creek, whose still waters wind without fuss between bands of untouched forest. The yellow pine and moss-draped cypress spread their shadows over quiet inlets; the splash of a fish or the chirp of a bird is the only sound.

Below the Waccamaw begin the life-abundant marshes, which stretch almost unending until they meld with the Florida beaches. This is, or was, rice country where great plantations spread their acreage, and Georgetown was the commercial capital. Rice cultivation was a labor-intensive business, and the end of slavery marked the beginning of its decline in South Carolina. The deathblow came when hurricane-driven salt water flooded the fields early in the last century, and there was not enough cheap labor left to restore them.

One does not think of a lifestyle generally associated with the antebellum South extending into the twentieth century, but such was the case on the rice plantations. The black workers planted and reaped in the same fields where their slave ancestors had labored. Their lives were not dissimilar. Of her father's land, which had been in the family five generations when she grew up at Rice Hope Plantation, Mrs. Margaret Morris recalled just a few years ago:

"They all lived on the plantation. They had their own chapel and their own minister came and held services for them."

And there was a slave burying ground where the horse her grandfather had ridden in the Civil War was interred as well.

"There was a lot of social life on the plantation. We'd have ten or fifteen people for dinner; nobody thought about the number. It was just a pleasant time for everybody to get together.

"We lived well on the plantation. It was pretty much self-sustaining. We always had cows and chickens and horses.

"We had two boys whose business it was to go seining every day with a wide net with big poles at each end. My heavens, we always had shrimp, crab, flounder — every fish you could think of. We ate lots of seafood."

When the flood came, the family moved to a smaller plantation inland to raise cotton. Today both plantations exemplify the changes that came over this area of the South. Rice Hope is shared cooperatively by several couples from the North, and the cotton fields inland have been made into a country club.

Georgetown's old houses are a quaint anachronism in a town that now sports a steel mill and a paper mill, but farther south along the Waterway lovely old McClellanville sleeps away the ages. Shrimpers line its docks, and great oak trees festooned with moss line its dusty streets. Friendly dogs accompany a stranger's walking tour, and through the gathering dusk the lights of the shingle church, stately in its simplicity, beckon to the passerby.

Then there is Charleston, a gracious lady in a picture hat with a twinkle in her eye. Early West Indian settlers gave her a lilt; French Huguenots, a Gallic charm; English Puritans and Scottish covenanters, a certain stolidity.

Adding a bit of seasoning were Hessian soldiers left over from the Revolutionary War, as well as refugees from the French and Haitian revolutions and the Irish rebellion. At the end of the eighteenth century, the largest Jewish community in America added to Charleston's rich life.

Commanding the great estuary where the Ashley and Cooper rivers flow into the Atlantic, she has been a major port since her founding as Charles Towne in 1670. Much of the world's rice, cotton, and indigo sailed from her docks.

Her favors have been fought for. As remote as it seems, the War of the Spanish Succession spilled into her harbor in 1706; she had just completed her first fortifications in time to beat back the French flotilla.

One of the earliest engagements of the Revolutionary War was the British fleet's attempt to capture Charleston, and the Civil War's first engagement, of course, was the Confederate attack on Fort Sumter at the harbor's mouth.

Charleston was under siege for most of both wars. The British occupied it for much of the Revolutionary War. In the Civil War the Union Army was in sight of the city's steeples in 1862, but her garrison held out until it was evacuated toward the war's close during Sherman's drive to the sea. The port was blockaded from the beginning, and Union gunners pounded its harbor works from land and sea for most of the final two years of the war.

There is no more interesting street in America than South Battery Street on Charleston's harbor front.

It was here that the guns were ranged that answered the British and the Union, and it was here, from their mansions' second- and third-floor porches, that the bemused citizenry watched the red flashes and heard the thunder as the Confederacy fired on Fort Sumter. None could foresee that the hostilities thus begun would not end until 646,392 lives had been forfeited and the South laid waste.

Charleston's riches have flowed from adversity. The city's commerce was disrupted by the War of 1812 and destroyed by the Civil War to the extent it could not afford to tear down its old buildings to keep up with the times. Today these homes and commercial buildings are lovingly preserved to provide the nation a jewel of a colonial city. It is a city of brick and pastel mansions. Many are turned discreetly so their sides are to the street, and the porches face gardens behind iron lace gates.

From Charleston south the Waterway winds a serpentine path through country so sparsely settled that hours can pass without sight of human habitation. But where humans are absent, wildlife teems. The endless salt marshes, their mud fringes exposed at low tide, are alive with birds.

The tall saw grass has also sheltered other forms of wildlife. Pirates and blockade runners found a refuge there and, in more recent years, rum and dope runners, too. There is a fishing town where, modern legend has it, half the population has faced narcotic charges, and up one river an entire fleet of shrimp boats lies idle under Coast Guard impoundment.

On the other hand, there is Church Creek, which locals still run to meet their Sunday obligations. At Church Flats the tides meet. It is well to go to church on the tide and return on the ebb.

Down that lonely stretch and around a bend rises, on its gentle bluff like a mirage, one of America's great living museums, South Carolina's Beaufort.

Its waterfront has been imaginatively reconstructed. Its grassy promenade is redolent with magnolia and wisteria and is furnished, in an ingenious touch, with old-fashioned porch swings. One can sit and imagine the sailing ships that once carried a great commerce from the city.

A short walk behind the park lies block after block of Beaufort's treasure: more than a score of mansions, under towering oaks hung with moss, on whose wide verandas and sweeping lawns the citizens once traded gossip and alarms of the Revolutionary and Civil wars.

The sweet smell of the South, of camellias and azaleas, clings to Beaufort's ancient and historic buildings: one of the nation's oldest churches, built of ballast rocks in 1724, whose cemetery tombstones served the occupying Union forces as operating tables; the house where the first Ordinance of Secession was drawn up to take South Carolina out of the Union and lead the procession of states into the Confederacy; the mansion where the aging Marquis de Lafayette stayed on his triumphal visit to the nation he helped save; and its oldest surviving house, built in 1717 with musket slits in the foundation to discourage raiding Indians.

Beaufort lives an anachronism for it is on the northern edge of the huge Parris Island reservation where U.S. marines learn the art of modern war. The Waterway skirts the island, but at least here, in contrast to the marines' Camp LeJeune up north of Wilmington, the run is on occasion interrupted by picketboats and uniformed men in watchtowers warning with their red flags of artillery practice and the danger of errant shells. Not the marines, presumably, but some other droll admirer of Napoleon named Parris's adjoining island St. Helena and one a little farther on in the Savannah River, Elba.

In 1562, at the mouth of the Beaufort River, Jean Ribault established one of the earliest French settlements on the Atlantic Coast. He found it "one of the greatest and fairest havens in the world, where without danger all the ships in the world might be harbored."

It became known as Port Royal, one of the deepest natural harbors south of the Chesapeake, and a major phosphate shipping port. Here was launched history's greatest amphibious landing up until World War II.

A Union armada landed thirteen thousand soldiers and marines to take the Confederate's Fort Walker on the heel of Hilton Head Island. They turned it into a naval base and built miles of earthworks along the shore to protect it. As the later headquarters of the Union's Department of the South, Fort Walker became a bustling town, only to fade afterward into oblivion.

The Yankees were merely the latest visitors to Hilton Head. Before them the Spanish and French landed their longboats in the sixteenth century, and the British came in the seventeenth century. A few thousand years earlier, according to archaeologists, another civilization left an intriguing legacy. In the center of the island's pristine forest reserve stands a mysterious mound of oyster shells and animal bones, 150 feet across and rising several feet high. Its origins and its purpose are unknown. Believers in such things might see in the mound a target for ancient visitors from another planet.

Hilton Head today is thirty thousand acres of playground, typifying plush resorts on Sea Island, Amelia Island, and other offshore islands from the Carolinas to the Florida coast. Carefully preserved by its ecologically aware developers are thousands of acres of virgin forest and marsh where wildfowl breed and alligators swim.

Across broad Calibogue Sound (pronounced Calie-bogie) lies Daufuskie, and then beyond, Savannah. This charming vamp is the saucy younger sister of the great cities of the Southeast Coast. It was half a century after Charles Towne was founded that General James Edward Oglethorpe landed his three dozen families at the bend of the river to establish the thirteenth British colony in America. Tucked under his arm were plans already drawn in London for his capital.

It was a case of city planning that worked. Today the pattern of squares, around which the courtly regency and federal mansions face each other across flower-blazoned parks, marks Savannah's unique charm.

The city's long-neglected waterfront has been restored. Old brick and stone warehouses, in which cotton and naval stores once were kept, have been turned into hotels, restaurants, galleries, and shops. Hard against the bluff, the four- and five-story buildings join the city across a series of iron and wooden bridges.

One can see Savannah's parasol-twirling beauties of another age promenading across her squares and, down along River Street, hear the sailor's jackboots echoing on the cobblestones.

December is a poor month in Savannah's history. In December

1793 the British besieged and captured it; almost on that anniversary seventy-one years later, Union forces did the same. Savannah was the target of General Sherman's drive to the sea that split the South and spelled the Confederacy's doom.

Savannah helped write our history. From there Oglethorpe mounted his two unsuccessful attempts to capture St. Augustine from the Spanish; there John Wesley briefly preached his new Methodism (and ran afoul of Oglethorpe); there, on the plantation of the late General Nathanael Greene, Eli Whitney invented the cotton gin; and from there sailed to Liverpool the first steamboat to cross the Atlantic, appropriately named *Savannah*.

Savannah is the gateway to Georgia's Golden Isles, which shelter from Atlantic winds the Waterway as it twists south through the marshes. Resorts flourish on the islands, but so does history. Sea Island gave the world a fine, strong, and lustrous cotton fiber that bears its name. The British built their largest and probably most costly fort in North America on St. Simon's Island. Fort Frederica, like Savannah, was a planned community, designed as a model English village, its settlers all carefully selected. They eschewed the log cabins of the frontier, and the settlement was built in the old-country style of sawn timbers, brick, and tabby. Fire ravaged the town in 1758, but its remains are preserved as a national monument.

Cumberland, most southerly and largest of Georgia's Golden Isles, once was the almost exclusive preserve of Andrew Carnegie. The ruins of his mansion, Dungeness, now are a centerpiece of an otherwise wild national park, complete with rattlesnakes and cottonmouth moccasins.

From here deep into Florida, where the condominium parade begins, it is a wonder that the Waterway doesn't still run red from the blood spilled by Spanish, French, English, and Indians as they fought to claim this favored land.

Juan Ponce de León came in peace, seeking fortune and, purely incidentally, the fabled fountain of youth. His calendar said it was *Pascua Florida* (Easter's Feast of Flowers), 1513, when he first sighted the sun-drenched beach, and it's been Florida ever since.

For almost a century no part of the American coast was to see such intensively cruel and ferocious activity as did that sixty-mile section between what is now Florida's northernmost city, Fernandina Beach, and Matanzas Inlet, just south of St. Augustine.

The first French colony, Fort Caroline, established in 1564 at the mouth of the St. Johns River, suffered a fate characteristic of this bloody century. Barely a year old, it was raided by the Spanish, who later at Matanzas Inlet put to death its population "not as Frenchmen but as Lutherans."

France mounted a three-ship fleet of revenge that recaptured what the Spanish now called San Mateo, and they put to death every Spaniard. Legend says the French left them lying under a tablet that read they were executed "not as Spaniards, but as traitors, robbers, and murderers."

Of all the would-be colonies, only St. Augustine, built in 1565, survived the fury, although it was often attacked. Today it is the oldest surviving European settlement in the United States and, of course, a tourist center where visitors can visit the dungeons and walk the battlements of the mighty fort that met French and, later, British assaults. Significant ancient history is mostly left behind as the Waterway punches its way between the hotels and motels, mansions and cottages, and the big cities and small towns that line the Florida beaches, presenting collectively the greatest or, at least, the longest resort center in the world.

However, the Waterway voyage still is blessed occasionally by great natural beauty and even future history. There are said to be seven hundred species of fish in these Florida waters. The nation's first wildlife sanctuary, Pelican Island, between New Smyrna and Vero beaches, hosts the endangered brown pelican, wood ibis, white ibis, egrets, double-crested cormorants, and Louisiana herons. Strange mammals known as manatees at times poke their brown snouts above the surface to test the busy human environment, which threatens their existence.

The past and the future cohabit Merritt Island in the long and wide Indian River, which carries the Waterway 120 miles behind the barrier beach from Cape Canaveral to St. Lucie. The island is a 25,000-acre wildlife refuge, harboring eagles and vultures, pelicans, wading birds, gulls, terns, and sea turtles, armadillos, alligators, and bobcats.

It is also the world's first and, so far, only Moonport, from which humans departed to explore that distant orb and from which the first

Pelicans and Shrimpers

space commuter, the shuttle, is launched. Its launch towers and the Vertical Assembly Building, where rockets and spaceships are mated for their fiery takeoff, are starkly silhouetted for the passing boatman. At launch time, the broad river provides a vantage point for a fleet of anchored vessels of every ilk, from canoe to oceangoing palace.

A few years ago, on the beach below Cape Canaveral at Sebastian Inlet, one of the great treasure finds of modern times was made. There, in 1715, a storm drove aground an entire Spanish fleet carrying gold and silver home from the New World. A salvage party from St. Augustine recovered what it could reach, but millions of dollars of treasure lay buried in the offshore sands until the middle of the twentieth century, when a beachcomber kicked up pieces of eight and followed the trail to the submerged wrecks.

Not so lucky have been those who for years have explored the beaches and waters at the inlet of Boca Raton. Legend has it that Blackbeard buried, or perhaps lost to unkindly seas, some of his loot from the Spanish galleons. Skin divers have turned up a relic or two, and a few pieces of eight have been uncovered in the sand, but the bulk of the treasure, if there is one, eludes the searchers.

The Florida Waterway is dotted with other treasures: modern artifacts such as the opulent mansion at Palm Beach built by the Florida developer Henry Flagler; the farm equipment tycoon James Deering's palace of Viscaya on Biscayne Bay; and the resort hotel at Boca Raton built by the dazzling architect Addison Mizner, who envisioned it as the centerpiece of a new Venice.

Mizner's dream collapsed with the great crash of 1929, but there already was building another Venice — Fort Lauderdale. It had a natural advantage as the New River coursed down its center. The river and other tributaries now offer more than three hundred miles of canals, most of them navigable by boats of luxury size.

Ponce de León supposedly explored the New River. Certainly the Spanish settled here where Tequesta Indians, long before Christ, had gathered from dugout canoes the region's bounty — shellfish, sea turtles, birds, palmetto berries, sea grapes, and coco plums.

The fort that Major William Lauderdale built during Florida's fierce Seminole wars gave the city its name. Twenty-nine thousand sail- and powerboats make their home here, augmented in season by thousands of visiting boats. All the skill of a New York taxi driver often is needed to navigate the Waterway.

Fort Lauderdale is part of the waterfront megalopolis that is almost unending from Palm Beach to Miami. The Waterway runs behind the mangrove swamp from which Miami Beach's four hundred hotels now rise until they run out of beach at Biscayne Bay.

Key Biscayne marches at the head of the 150-mile-long procession of tropical islands that sweep southwestward to Key West. The larger, outer islands are themselves protected by offshore reefs. Tarpon are plentiful, and the fast-running, unpredictable bonefish roam the broad and shallow Biscayne and Florida Bays behind these barrier islands.

Mangrove and palms rise out of the dead coral that forms the islands, and a thousand flowers, whose seeds have floated there on wind or wave or been carried by wandering seabirds, perfume the air.

Only in the Keys can the United States boast a living coral reef. It has been made into a national underseas park to protect its 50 kinds of coral and 650 varieties of dainty, brilliant, gross, and ugly fish. Below the surface, a nine-foot-high bronze statue, *Christ of the Deep*, greets divers glorying in the glass-clear water.

Only in the Keys can be found a miniature, dog-sized variety of deer. Six hundred of these refugees from a Disney movie, known not unexpectedly as Key deer, live under government protection on Big Pine Key.

Threatened bald eagles, peregrine falcons, and brown pelicans have their own preserve, and all the islands are atwitter with birds that come like tourists for the winter season.

The island pearls are strung together by forty-two bridges — one engineering miracle is seven miles long. They carry U.S. 1 to join the Waterway at the southernmost city of the continental United States, its only truly tropical one.

Key West is American, but it also is Cuban, Bahamian, Bermudian, and West Indian. It has taken something in its people and its ambiance from each of its progenitors — Spanish conquistadores, pirates, Caribbean fishermen, and the American Navy, which sent forth from here the battleship *Maine* on its fateful ninety-mile crossing to Havana.

Like Key Biscayne, the city's early fortune came from the sea — in some cases, at least, deliberately lured to shore by wreckers whose false lights confused sailors, who sent their valuable cargoes crashing onto the shoals.

The now greatly outnumbered Key West natives proudly call themselves "conchs" after that ubiquitous mollusk. Many live in houses their grandfathers had built with the aid of itinerant ships' carpenters, using heart pine held tightly together with wooden pegs.

Key West slumbers through the hot midday, shutters closing out the sun that manages to penetrate the clustering poinciana and bougainvillea, and the breadfruit, coconut palms, and Spanish limes.

The island's main thoroughfare, Duvall Street, has the distinction of running its fourteen blocks from the Atlantic Ocean to the Gulf of Mexico and sporting an exotic nightlife.

John James Audubon turned out much of his famous work on American birds in a house that remains largely as he left it in 1832. The broad-verandaed house that Ernest Hemingway shared with a plethora of cats is a haven for tourists who are greeted by those felines' lineal descendants.

Key West celebrates its glorious sunset with an impromptu festival each evening on Mallory Square. Lying offshore, the yachtsman exults with the city in a sight that for most of a thousand miles down history's Waterway has been hidden behind the continent called America.

The Gulf Coast

THE GULF COAST HAS MUCH TO offer the cruising yachtsman, from the teeming waters of Florida's endangered Everglades to the barrier beaches of Texas, rich with wild bird life, including the winter home of the last surviving whooping cranes.

The Gulf is one of the nation's great sportfishing grounds with record catches of seemingly everything that swims out there.

Florida's burgeoning west coast, from Naples on the south to St. Petersburg on the north, certainly must rank as one of the nation's richest stretches of beach, resident by resident and mansion by mansion. In fact, at least until the birth of California's Silicon Valley, Naples had the reputation of having more millionaires per capita than any other city and more golf courses than any other city east of the Rockies.

The area is dotted with some of the nation's great houses, now fascinating museums, notably those of Thomas Edison and the circus man John Ringling. Edison designed and supervised the construction of every square foot of his vast houses and laboratory. Ringling's thirty-two-room mansion was patterned after the Doge's Palace in Venice.

Farther north are two communities whose early settlers imparted to them a character of their own. Tampa and its environs is now a metropolis, but within it is the area that once was Ybor City, where Cubans settled to make cigars. The mid-nineteenth-century district is well preserved, and some cigars are still hand-rolled there. And a little further north is Tarpon Springs, where the Greeks came and have stayed to dive for sponges.

As St. Petersburg, a lovely tropical city and a major yachting center, is the capital of the empire of beaches, Tarpon Springs is the centerpiece of a network of small rivers that lead to the dazzlingly clear springs of that region on the coast before the great bend to the Panhandle. Deep-draft boats may have trouble reaching them, but those incredible springs and the fabulous gardens around them reward the effort.

Behind West Florida's beaches are many exotic gardens and jungle parks, and just outside Fort Myers is the country's largest stand of virgin bald cypress trees and its largest nesting rookery of wood storks.

Up beyond Tarpon Springs lies a paradise for divers less specialized than those strong-lunged young men who dive for sponges. It is part of the Gulf Islands National Seashore off Florida's Panhandle between Pensacola and Panama City. Offshore from the miles of unspoiled beaches, there are more than forty artificial reefs of sunken ships — old windjammers, barges, an oil rig, even army tanks. There's a ninety-foot tug and the battleship USS *Massachusetts*, one of our first battleships of the then new "Steel Navy." She was commissioned just in time to see service blockading Cuba during the Spanish-American War. She ended her life ignominiously in the early 1920s as a target vessel for coastal artillery off Pensacola.

Farther along the coast, up the mighty Mississippi, the classic antebellum cities of Mobile and New Orleans beckon. One discovers at Mobile that the first great Mardi Gras parades were here, not in New Orleans, just part of the colorful history of the Gulf Coast and, particularly, of those two picturesque communities. They hosted three of the nation's most significant battles.

In the War of 1812 the Battle of New Orleans dealt the final blow to the English attempt to regain America. Actually the American victory at arms, led by the redoubtable General Andrew Jackson, had nothing to do with winning the war. It was important, however, in raising the morale and boosting the confidence of the young American nation.

Because of the molasses-like pace of early-nineteenth-century communications, the battle actually was fought two weeks after the British had surrendered with the Treaty of Ghent. Andy Jackson's victory also didn't hurt his later successful bid for the nation's presidency.

In the Civil War, New Orleans played a far more important role in our history than Jackson's postbellum victory there. Fairly early in the war, in 1862, the North's Admiral David Farragut in a daring maneuver captured New Orleans, one of the Confederacy's major supply ports.

In August 1864 Farragut struck again, dealing a crushing blow to the already waning fortunes of the Confederacy. At Mobile Bay he broke through what the South's navy thought was its impenetrable line of forts and torpedo boats to destroy much of the Confederacy's navy. It was there that Farragut gave Navy lore one of its lasting declarations of heroic bravado: "Damn the torpedoes, full speed ahead."

The part that pirates played is scarcely incidental to the story of the Battle of New Orleans. The so-called Prince of Pirates, Jean Laffite, was celebrated as a hero along with General Jackson.

Laffite's origins in France were unknown, but he was educated as well as handsome, well spoken, and well tailored — a gentleman, in other words. In a sense, he was more a smuggler than a pirate. From his base on Grand Terre Island, in the bayou country south of New Orleans, he commissioned pirates to bring their looted goods to him for sale in New Orleans. When the United States banned the importation of slaves, in 1808, he added them to his long list of smuggled goods.

Legitimate merchants tired of his competition, and he was arrested and his Grand Terre base destroyed. Nonetheless he turned down a British offer of a commission and a fortune in cash to lead their planned attack on New Orleans in the War of 1812. Instead he advised authorities in New Orleans of the British plan and led a small army of his Grand Terre brigands to join General Jackson in defense of the city. President Madison pardoned him and his followers for their acts of piracy.

His Grand Terre base gone, Laffite sailed for three years looking for a new base and finally settled on the virtually deserted Galveston Island in the then Spanish colony that became Texas. Three years later he moved on to Mujeres Island off Yucatán, Mexico, where he died a few years later.

Disillusioned and unappreciated as he felt in departing Louisiana, the state now honors him with a monument and a town that bears his name.

Laffite's fame was rivaled by that of another Gulf-based pirate, the fabled Gasparilla. He was wellborn in Spain, a graduate of its naval academy as something of a genius. In 1732, when he was only twenty-

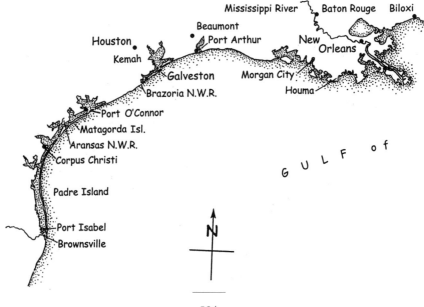

six, his daredevil leadership at sea against Tripoli pirates gained him promotion to admiral.

Admiral José Gaspar, as he was then known, was posted as naval aide to King Charles III's court. His wit and charm beguiled the court, including, unfortunately for Gaspar, a princess of the royal household. One thing led to another, as happens in such cases, and Gaspar fled Madrid, organized a bunch of convicts, stole a navy bark, and launched a pirate career that brought him to the coast of the Gulf of Mexico.

He was one of the most successful, and most murderous and ruthless, pirates of that bloody period. So large did his enterprise grow that he needed a substantial land base with warehouses for his shiploads of loot, and he picked an island in Charlotte Harbor on Florida's west coast. He named it after himself, Gasparilla, and he called the little town that became his home and headquarters Boca Grande. He also gave to other nearby islands the names they bear today — Sanibel,

Cayo Costa, and Useppa (a corruption of Josefa, as he named it).

Named by him as well was the island of Captiva, which probably bears a dark history indeed. It is the Spanish feminine form of the word for captive, and there is every reason to believe it is where he kept the women from the ships he plundered — the unfortunate ones whom he did not immediately put to death but kept as sex slaves for himself and his band of cutthroats.

We are entitled to wonder what Gasparilla would think if he knew that today, more than two centuries later, one of the great annual festivals along the Gulf of Mexico shores is named for him and celebrates the lore of piracy.

The history of the Gulf Coast also features the most destructive hurricane ever to strike an American city — the great wind and flood that devastated Galveston, Texas, in 1900. The bustling city was to a large degree destroyed, and six thousand persons lost their lives.

The Gulf has its nasty side, weatherwise. It is distinctly different from the great oceans. Basking in the less harsh climate of the tropics, it has a languid quality and is not as frequently disturbed as the oceans, but it can be deadly when its temper rises in hurricane season. Even normally, with its comparatively shallow depth, it can become particularly ornery with a vicious chop when the wind rises.

These seas are constantly at work modifying the Gulf coast. The western Florida coast is reasonably stable, but there are substantial geological changes along the Mississippi and Louisiana coasts. Barrier beaches are building up as storms drag sand off the beaches and pile them up on the first shallow obstruction offshore. As the barrier islands build, the mainland beaches recede. It is not a notable danger in a human time frame, but in geological time, measured in centuries and eons, it is happening rather quickly.

There also is subsidence along the Texas and Louisiana coasts that occasionally causes some trouble for low-lying delta areas that barely peek above the surface in the first place. Offshore, particularly off the Louisiana and East Texas coasts, there are cities of oil platforms in four to five hundred feet of water on the continental shelf. Their lights almost resemble cities at night — or perhaps a field of football stadiums. It is good that they are visible to night-traveling cruising boats, but the light pollution renders the area scarcely one in which to study the stars or admire the moon.

Now there is intense deep drilling far out from the shelf on the continental slope, the rigs sending their pipes down where they pierce the bottom at nine thousand feet or more, almost two miles below the surface.

The oil companies claim, and not a few fishermen agree, that the long legs of the oil platforms actually create the effect of an artificial reef and are a great lure to many species of fish.

Frightening for sailors new to the Gulf are the commercial long-line fishing boats. Incredibly their long lines trail out six to ten miles from the boats. They are buoyed occasionally, and they are fifteen to thirty feet deep where the swordfish are. They are not a real threat to even the largest deep-draft sailboat except as a psychological hazard.

The Gulf is lined for much of its distance by the Intracoastal Waterway, a dredged canal through bays and bayous for one thousand miles, from the Florida Panhandle almost to the Mexican border. It is heavy with commercial traffic of huge tugs and their tows, and except for its comparative safety and its access to some of the South's loveliest towns it isn't exactly a boater's heaven.

Power cables, locks, bridges, and cable ferries present a seldom relieved challenge. In the spring floods as the rivers pour out into the

Gulf, their five-knot currents pose an additional hazard. And large shrimp boats with an astonishingly shallow draft of only two feet present another problem as they rest calmly at anchor and lure unsuspecting deeper-draft cruising boats to an unpleasant grounding.

Of those handsome and historic towns reached by the Waterway, the oak-lined streets and white frame homes of Mississippi's Port Gibson are typical. Port Gibson was made famous by General Grant's statement as he passed through on his way to Vicksburg in 1863 that Port Gibson "is too beautiful to burn."

Biloxi, the first capital of the Louisiana Territory, is a delightful antebellum city, now a bustling tourist center. Its outstanding historic treasure is beautifully preserved Beauvais, the last home of Jefferson Davis, the president of the Confederacy.

Undoubtedly the Waterway's most scenic passage is that along the tortuous route through the Mississippi Delta's bayous below New Orleans. They are a maze of streams of moss-hung cypress and minefields of cypress stumps. The Waterway itself is an interesting but cluttered confusion of drilling rigs, oil barges, shrimp boats, and local cayaques. Deceptively pretty annoyances here are the hyacinths so thick they threaten to choke a boat's propellers.

The route winds past innumerable little canals leading to the always present landing at the end of the only street in the creole villages. Morgan City is the bayou country's capital, an island that is home port to more than a thousand fishing boats as well as the location of a century-old marine supply store.

Besides providing us this most picturesque part of the Gulf coast, Louisiana is home to an important part of our colonial heritage.

The nation may have been founded by the Anglo-Saxon settlers along the Atlantic coast, but the Gulf states, discovered and settled by the Spanish and the French, gave it a diversity vital to its eventual strength. Indeed, that inevitable mixture of Spanish and French blood of the Gulf coast, along with the infusion of that of the African slaves, gave us one of our most distinctive and interesting ethnic groups — the Creoles, who have enriched the culture of Louisiana.

Along with the Cajuns, descendants of the French refugees the British drove from Acadia, the Creoles are still dominant in the bayou country. And the Creoles, of course, with some added spices from the Cajuns, have bestowed on New Orleans one of the world's great cuisines.

West of Louisiana along the coast the French influence peters out and the Spanish influence is minimal, buried by the robust pioneers, many from Kentucky, who defeated Mexico's army to establish the independent nation of Texas. For the whole of the nineteenth century, their commercial capital was Galveston. Until 1900 it was their financial center and Texas's most prosperous city. It ranked as one of the world's busiest cotton ports.

Land speculators flocked to Galveston and built imposing office buildings and elaborate mansions, most in the Victorian style. Then came the 1900 hurricane. And just as Galveston was beginning to recover, another, almost as disastrous storm hit in 1915.

The twin blows almost finished Galveston — that and the discovery of oil nearby. The surviving citizens of Galveston were just emerging from their temporary shelters in 1901 when the Spindletop oil field's Lucas Gusher blew in at neighboring Beaumont. It produced several thousand times more oil than any previous well. The pipeline from Spindletop terminated in Houston, and thus began that city's great growth, far eclipsing Galveston.

Galveston today, however, is a city enjoying revival. The Strand, the five-block-long, three-block-wide business area that once was

called the Wall Street of the Southwest, has been largely restored, as
have some magnificent mansions. And Galveston's natural benefits
include thirty-two miles of sandy beaches.

The city is justifiably proud of the community effort that restored
the 160-foot iron bark *Elissa*. Built in Scotland in 1877, she first visited
New York in 1884 and came back a century later to help celebrate the
Statue of Liberty's one hundredth birthday. She was magnificent that
day as she sailed into New York Harbor with all nineteen sails flying!

Galveston is one of the most important terminals on the Intracoastal Waterway, and it is the southern terminus of the busy shipping
route from Houston, fifty miles up Galveston Bay. That and the heavy
oceangoing traffic to and from its own two miles of piers render Galveston's surrounding waters something of a small boater's nightmare.
Sometimes a score or more large ships are anchored east of Galveston's
jetties, waiting to enter port.

Incidentally, despite the traffic, the stretch of the Intracoastal
from Galveston to nearby Port Arthur, Texas, is said to have the greatest
population of alligators on the Waterway.

Elissa *at Galveston*

Galveston Bay is big and shallow — thirty miles long, seventeen miles wide, and, on the average, eight feet deep. Boats can anchor anywhere except in the busy ship channels, but being that shallow, the Bay is a sucker for strong winds. A norther can lower the water level by three feet; a good stiff wind from the south can raise it three to six feet.

Along its western banks are the neighboring towns of Kemah, Seabrook, League City, and Nassau Bay, which together have the largest concentration of pleasure boats between Los Angeles and St. Petersburg.

Kemah is the entrance to something called Clear Lake. It seems to be a little cleaner now, but in my boyhood that was a classic misnomer. In the early part of the twentieth century, some people said it was so muddy you could walk on it. Now it is criss-crossed with channels that bring in the somewhat cleaner water of the bay. It is lined by mansions, luxurious condominiums, and developments that have been the homes of most of the nation's astronauts.

The Johnson Space Center — site of shuttle mission control, scientific development, and astronaut training and a major tourist attraction — is on its banks.

When I was a boy in Houston several score decades ago, Kemah was a sleepy little fishing port into which the shrimp and oyster boats came to unload their daily catch. It was a shrine that invited a frequent pilgrimage from Houston down the roads mostly paved with oyster shells. We bought those luscious big Gulf shrimp and oysters at fifteen cents a pint or twenty-five cents a quart. The system dictated that we buy the empty containers from a little stand at the edge of the dock and hold them out to the fishermen to fill.

For all its vast size, largest of the contiguous United States, Texas's coastline is relatively short — 450 miles, about a third of that which

Florida boasts. Scattered passes break the long, flat barrier islands that make up most of the shoreline. Behind the islands are bays that have played a big part in the growth of Texas industry and pleasure boating.

Those islands are famous for their bird life — literally thousands and thousands of them of many breeds. Together the islands form one of the nation's great sanctuaries for the feathered migrants, particularly Brazoria and Aransas national wildlife refuges. Aransas Refuge, near Port O'Conner, is the winter home of the world's surviving handful of whooping cranes. The cranes' fellow occupants of the refuge include wild turkeys, pelicans, egrets, spoonbills, warblers, and ducks.

Lengthy Padre Island, below Corpus Christi, is notable for a succession of seaside resorts that lure the birds as well as a few thousand college students for spring break. Aransas Pass to Corpus Christi may be the prettiest section of the Gulf coast, certainly the Texas portion thereof. It is a summer rendevous for artists, photographers, sailors, fishermen, and birdwatchers. When the kingfish are running, coming inshore in September and October, they can be caught right outside the jetties at Port Aransas. Aransas Pass also harbors one of the state's largest shrimping fleets and features a memorial honoring shrimpers lost at sea.

Corpus Christi is situated on its own bay, fifteen miles long and eleven miles wide, and its yachting facilities can't be beat for metropolitan convenience. They are right downtown on the city's handsome Shoreline Drive.

For the United States, Gulf coast boating activity effectively ends at Port Isabel, the last port before the border with Mexico and a major sportfishing center. The area holds the state records for blue marlin, bluefin tuna, mako shark, and tarpon.

Dashing as the big, deep-sea sportfishermen are, our heroes should be the commercial fishermen who venture out from our coasts. These valiant men, and the occasional woman, dare the oceans' murderous rages to help feed the nation. Their work is one of the poorest understood of all our industries, although the book *The Perfect Storm* and the movie made from it at the turn of the new century helped acquaint the public with its hazards.

The commercial deep-sea fishermen invest hundreds of thousands of dollars in their ships and their complicated fishing rigs. They also invest the lives of themselves and their crews in an occupation listed by the government as the nation's second most dangerous, after timber cutting. Their living is earned in a never-ceasing contest with nature, who at her foulest demands a tribute of ships and men.

They sail from all our coasts — the American coasts, as varied and as grand as any this globe of ours has to offer.

The West Coast

STAND OUT THERE ON THE LONELY rocks that form the promontory called Cape Flattery, and you'll probably be the first person in these lower forty-eight of the United States to feel the west wind. It can brush your cheek with a gentle kiss or knock you down with a heavyweight's punch.

Now, if the west wind is *truly* west, that is, right out of 270 degrees, your chances of being the first to feel its touch would be enhanced if you traveled thirteen miles south along this rugged Washington coast to a deserted place called Cape Alava. This spot actually is the westernmost point of the lower forty-eight, just a smidgin farther west than Cape Flattery — barely a minute of longitude, a geographical whisper of scarcely a mile.

But the west wind usually comes in to the coast just a little north of west, and that does hit Flattery first.

It is likely that you'll be alone out there at Flattery. No one lives there. It's Indian country, the Makah reservation, and there aren't any residents for four miles back east until you get to the fishing village of Neah Bay.

To get to Flattery from the main highway, you drive for miles over unmarked washboard lumber roads, through redolent pine and spruce and fir and past the ugly scars where it has been cut over.

You find your way by trial and error until finally, at a wide spot in the road, you see a sign that some kindly local has hand-lettered. It points to Cape Flattery. Dismounting, you hike for another mile or more along a barely perceptible trail, sweet with the smell of the

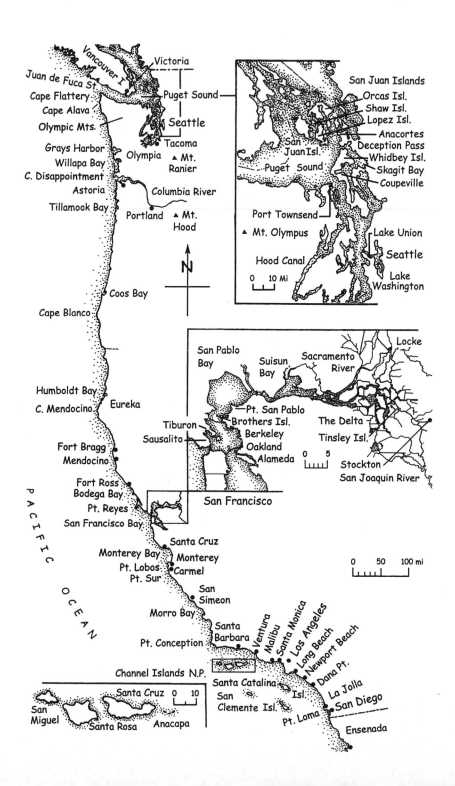

Victoria

Vancouver I.

Juan de Fuca St.
Cape Flattery
Cape Alava
Olympic Mts.
Grays Harbor
Willapa Bay
C. Disappointment
Astoria
Tillamook Bay

Puget Sound
Seattle
Olympia
Tacoma
▲ Mt.
Ranier
Columbia River
Portland   ▲ Mt.
              Hood

San Juan Islands
Orcas Isl.
Shaw Isl.
Lopez Isl.
Anacortes
Deception Pass
Whidbey Isl.
Skagit Bay
Coupeville

San
Juan Isl.
Puget Sound

Port Townsend

▲ Mt. Olympus

Hood Canal

Lake Union
Seattle
Lake
Washington

0   10 Mi

N

Coos Bay

Cape Blanco

Humboldt Bay
C. Mendocino   Eureka

Fort Bragg
Mendocino

Fort Ross
Bodega Bay
Pt. Reyes
San Francisco Bay

PACIFIC

OCEAN

San Pablo
Bay

Suisun
Bay

Sacramento
River

Locke

Pt. San Pablo
Brothers Isl.
Berkeley
Oakland
Alameda

Tiburon
Sausalito

The Delta

Tinsley Isl.

San Francisco

0   5

Stockton
San Joaquin River

Santa Cruz
Monterey Bay   Monterey
Pt. Lobos   Carmel
Pt. Sur

San
Simeon

Morro Bay

0   50   100 mi

Santa
Barbara

Pt. Conception

Ventura
Malibu
Santa Monica
Los Angeles
Long Beach
Newport Beach

Channel Islands N.P.

Santa Catalina
San
Clemente Isl.

Isl.

Dana Pt.

La Jolla
San Diego

Santa Cruz   0   10

San
Miguel   Santa Rosa   Anacapa

Pt. Loma

Ensenada

forest's freshness. You climb over fallen logs, stumble over the exposed root systems of the forest, slide down muddy inclines, and, with more difficulty, climb others. Then you hear the surf—or is that the wind rustling through the forest's canopy above?

And then, when you are about to give up in despair, light appears at the end of your bowered tunnel, and the trees open up like a stage curtain to reveal before you one of nature's spectaculars.

You walk onto the naked promontory jutting fifty yards out from the wooded cliffs. Two hundred feet below, the waves smash against the rocks and send their eddies curling into shore. Over there, on a tree jutting from the face of the bluff, an eagle warily watches these intruders. And in front, between you and Japan, is the small island a mile offshore, barely more than a rock outcropping, that is now the site of the Cape Flattery Lighthouse.

You can see clearly the little inlet in the lee side of the island from which the Tatoosh Indians a century ago launched their boats to go out and harvest the sea life then abundant in this country. Early explorers were impressed with the fancy blankets the Tatoosh made from the hair of dogs that they kept and clipped as they would sheep.

Here the Pacific must come to its decision. Most of it takes the right turn around Flattery and pushes on down our western coast. A smaller but still sizable portion carries on into what is called the Juan de Fuca Strait, named for the sixteenth-century Spanish explorer who first discovered this passage. De Fuca's description of the area was so imprecise, however, that the strait was not rediscovered until 1787 by a twenty-seven-year-old Boston fur trader named Charles Barkley.

Earlier, the vaunted English explorer Captain James Cook had tried to find Juan de Fuca's passage and had given up at its very entrance with a note in his log doubting de Fuca's description of the place. But

Cook did write that he was "flattered" by having found what he thought was a rather impressive inlet, and hence the name of the point.

Over to our right is Canada's magnificent Vancouver Island and now in back of us, past Mount Olympus, are the San Juan Islands and Puget Sound. Here is where we want to start any sailing trip along our western coast. The wind and the current are with us sailing south, and the ride is likely to be far more comfortable than slugging north with the wind in our face and the big Pacific rollers trying to push us down.

"Hell, man," one old sailor told me in San Diego, "the only way to sail from here to Puget Sound is to take a long tack out to Hawaii and then tack back."

That little jaunt — and some do it — would put 5,286 miles under your boat's bottom. The trip directly from Seattle in the north to San Diego in the south would come to 1,052 miles.

Even sailing south the voyage is, for the most part, along an unforgiving coast — cliffs and rocks ashore and the constant threat of sudden, violent storms at sea. This really isn't sailing country for cruising boats, at least not compared with the Atlantic coast, with its many wide and easily entered bays, its frequent harbors, and its long inland waterway.

This west coast, in fact, may be the longest water frontier in the world with the smallest number of natural harbors. The only totally natural ones are the bays at San Francisco and San Diego. There now are other harbors, but they either are man-made or, even with man's help, lie behind shifting sandbars that can frequently make an entry treacherous.

Actually, the Pacific coast is two coasts divided by a sort of atmospheric Mason-Dixon Line at Point Conception, midway down the California coast. The coast of northern California, Oregon, and Washington is lashed by northwest storms that are born far out at sea and have grown to be giants by the time they stride onto the continent. The coast, however, slides away southeasterly from Conception and, lying in the lee of the more violent northwesters, becomes gentle. The cliffs are less numerous, the beaches long and soft.

So, any sailing cruise along this coast should start at Puget Sound after the spring rains and in plenty of time to make it to Conception before the fall storms.

The only problem is that once one has sailed Puget Sound and the San Juan Islands, one may decide that paradise could offer no improvements. That decision would be wrong, of course. Nothing is perfect. The area does have an extraordinary amount of rainfall, the winters are not exactly tropical, and the summer winds, when the weather is fair, are likely to be sparse. But to note that is to quibble. Boating in the Pacific Northwest, in season, comes pretty close to perfection. And anyway, that lack of wind suits the fishermen. Everyone to his own!

Seattle is the capital of the region, and there is small wonder that its population is expanding a little faster than some of the old-timers would like. Perhaps only Sydney, Australia, among waterfront metropolises, can rival it for gracious living. A sizable portion of its daytime population commutes by ferry from the nearby islands, and while most

Ferry Puget Sound

of these commuters may have become blasé with their daily routines, to the tourist it is exciting to approach this sparkling city by water.

A narrow waterway connects the sound with thirty-eight-square-mile Lake Washington, where the wakes of hundreds of boats wrinkle the reflection of Mount Rainier, whose elegant snowy peak rises to the southeast.

The University of Washington campus is on the western side of Lake Washington, and its football stadium is on the bank. When the Huskies are playing at home, yachtsmen from Seattle and waterfront communities up and down the sound come to the game by boat with their purple-and-gold banners raised to the mast tops, anchoring and rafting dozens deep just outside the stadium gates.

Union Bay between the lake and the sound cuddles up to downtown Seattle, its pleasure-boat slips but an elevator ride and a few steps from office to dock. Much of this waterfront is lined with house-boats, four and five deep out into the channel.

Varying from the hippie to the substantial, most are one-story affairs, but some have added a second story. At some points piers stretch like sidewalks the length of the moorings, but at others the houseboats are simply rafted, and dwellers at the water's end cross the "front porches" of their neighbors to get ashore or back home.

With fireplace glowing and water lapping at the "foundation," they can be charmingly homey. When the great geographer-oceanographer Athlestan Spilhaus was the head of the official U.S. exhibit at Seattle's 1962 World's Fair, he scandalized the stodgier bureaucrats by preferring to spend most of his time in a houseboat rather than in the mansion provided him on Lake Washington.

A lock to control the water's flow from Puget Sound has made possible Seattle's inner harbor. Navigating the lock provides the yachtsman with one of life's little thrills. Tugs and their lumber barges, inter-island freighters, excursion boats, fishing boats, and sailboats jockey to hold their places against the swift current and to avoid each other until the lockkeeper's green light signals them to come ahead.

Keeping the boat in position and free of collision is a task requiring extreme concentration, and yet in the midst of the confusion there is a distracting element. Huge salmon, just having completed the last step up the neighboring artificial ladder that helps them get upstream to spawn, leap for joy or relief or for some other anthropomorphic reason. They are so close, it seems that they'll land in the cockpit with you. Even for the old-timers, this is cause for excitement.

In fact, the old-timers seem to get as much of a kick out of wildlife up here as the astounded neophyte. It is something that sets these northwesterners apart. They all appear to be keen naturalists, and as often as they sail among the wildlife, they identify with delight (or argue with gusto about) the birds and fish and landlocked animal life that thrive in the region.

More serious thrills wait on the other side of the lock. By treaty the Indians are permitted to catch the salmon there, and their gill nets stretched across the narrow exit to the sound make it almost impassable and a nerve-racking trip. A fouled keel or propellor in that fast-running current could create an ornery affair.

Although the buildup in the area seems to accelerate constantly, the Pacific Northwest still is almost virgin country compared with the much longer developed East. After all, the area was explored for the first time in the late eighteenth century when British, American, and Spanish sailors were almost bumping into each other to investigate this great land, which had just been opened up by the discovery of the passage at Cape Flattery.

And it wasn't until almost the middle of the nineteenth century, at a time when the cities of the Northeast already were burgeoning, that bands of courageous settlers from Missouri pushed their wagons and portaged their canoes to a landing at what is now Olympia, Washington, down at the southwestern corner of Puget Sound.

One of the leaders of the little pioneer band that settled on the spot where the Olympia Brewery stands today was an African-American, George Washington Bush. Not many of his race followed, however; today African-Americans constitute only 4 percent of the population of Oregon and Washington, one of the lowest percentages in America.

The Bush party, in its two-year trek along the rivers and through the wilderness and over the mountains to reach the Oregon Territory, luckily avoided serious Indian attacks; on the contrary, one of the most dramatic episodes in their daily adventures showed the other side of the Indians.

An Indian carried off the baby of David and Tallitha Kindred one day. "Kidnapped into a life of slavery," the little band wailed. But the next day the Indian rode back to their camp to return the baby, now decked out in buckskin jacket and boots that his village had provided.

You can sail into the front yard of Washington's fine old capitol building at Olympia by dodging a hundred old pilings and threading a narrow channel over the mud flats.

Up at the top of Puget Sound is the entrance to Hood Canal, which is a thousand times prettier than that name would suggest. Narrow and wild, huddled under the lee of the Olympic Mountains, its waters seem warmer than the sound, conducive to swimming, and its gentle banks are loaded with rhododendrons in such profusion that they won special notice from the botanist who accompanied the British explorer George Vancouver there in 1793.

You may remember Hood Canal for those dramatic pictures taken some years ago of the bridge being whipped by violent winds until it heaved and twisted itself to destruction and collapsed into the water below.

Glorious as the canal and the sound are for sailing and fishing — perch, trout, bottom fish, crabs, mussels, oysters, salmon, always salmon — and for the lovely coves and spectacular views on Seattle's doorstep, the storied boating of the San Juan Islands wonderland still is a one- or two-day sail away up north.

For better sailing we can take the windward side of Whidbey Island and make a stop at Port Townsend, almost the epitome of the coastal and river towns all over the Northwest whose boom days of lumber and fish canneries have passed but which have found a new appeal as tourist attractions and recreational centers. Port Townsend lends itself well to that. The substantial Victorian homes of its lumber, fishing, and mercantile barons preside at the top of its sharp cliffs, looking down on the restored hotels and commercial buildings of its waterfront business street.

From Port Townsend to the nearest point of the San Juans is barely twenty miles, but it can be three hours of some pretty wild and woolly sailing. The currents flowing around Vancouver Island and the San Juans and down the sound and Hood here meet to create their own confusion, compounded by the west wind rushing down the Juan de Fuca Strait at twenty knots or more. Wild and woolly, yes, but spirited and probably the best sailing in the region, for despite the idyllic boating everywhere here, the winds in the lee of the high forested banks and between the islands naturally are likely to be light and, at best, fluky.

That rough patch off Port Townsend sends many smaller boats, particularly the powerboats, on an inside passage from Seattle to the islands—up on the lee side of Whidbey, through Saratoga Passage, Skagit Bay, and unique and picturesque Squinomish Channel into Padilla Bay. This route also has the advantage of being on the more attractive side of thirty-six-mile-long Whidbey Island, with its expansive meadows and its display of wildflowers.

Whidbey's first settler was one Isaac Ebey, who gave his name to a lot of the features on the island. He met a rather gruesome end one night when, awakened by his dog, Rover, he arose to investigate a noise outside the family cabin and ran into a band of marauding Indians. They killed and decapitated him and took his head as a trophy. Ebey's good friend Captain Charles Dodd, who as a Hudson Bay Company skipper traded among the savage Indians of Alaska's southeast coast, made guarded and judicious inquiries until, two years after the slaying, Dodd found Ebey's head and returned it to be buried with the rest of him in the family plot.

At the top of Whidbey Island, one of the Northwest's boating experiences awaits—a trip through Deception Pass. This deep defile is just a mile long and barely 150 yards wide, and when running full, the waters gush and tumble through it at a hefty eight knots.

It is said that in the days of sail, only one skipper ever dared bring a full-rigger through Deception Pass. That was Captain Thomas Coupe in 1852. He later settled on Whidbey, and Coupeville today is one of the island's most charming old towns.

The insignificance of humans measured against nature overwhelms us as we navigate this narrow pass with its steep cliffs enfolding us. High overhead a graceful bridge arches over the pass.

Deception Pass was named by Vancouver, who might have been impressed with its appearance but not with its potential as a water route to anywhere. He already had charted it as a scenic but worthless inlet when his master, Joseph Whidbey, on a scouting foray, discovered its true nature. Vancouver got out his eraser and, presumably good-naturedly, named it Deception.

It is remarkable how many geographical features along the west coast, many far more prominent than Deception Pass, were missed by the early explorers. Sir Francis Drake sailed right by the Golden Gate and missed the chance to discover San Francisco Bay (some of his apologists blame an impenetrable fog). The Spanish explorer Sebastián Vizcaíno also couldn't find it. Captain James Cook missed the wide entrance to the Columbia River and, on the threshold of the wondrous land to the east, turned back after barely sailing into Juan de Fuca Strait.

In these early maritime adventures there is other perverse satisfaction for us modern sailors. The log of Lieutenant Charles Wilkes, whose naval expedition thoroughly exploring Puget Sound in 1838 helped solidify the United States' claim to the area, tells of what must have been a severe embarrassment to that proud and autocratic mariner.

Trying to get underway from a Whidbey Island anchorage where Port Orchard is now, and surely eager to impress an observer from the rival Hudson Bay Company aboard for the first day of an unprecedented visit, Wilkes in his 780-ton sloop, *Vincennes*, instead fouled one anchor and swung into the sand off Whidbey Island. Wilkes finally worked the vessel free, but just as he was getting underway, the other anchor let loose and snagged him again. Some friends of mine are adept at the Wilkes Maneuver.

(It may be unfair to name this bit of unfortunate seamanship after Wilkes. Although almost universally disliked by his men for his haste in criticizing what they frequently thought were his own mistakes and for his almost equal quickness in ordering the lash for offenders, he still named many of the features his party discovered after his officers and men and none for himself.)

Deception Pass leads into Skagit Bay and Skagit Bay into Squinomish Channel, which provides the ten-mile route through to Padilla Bay and Anacortes, the pleasure-boat launching pad for the San Juans. The Squinomish at its bottom end is a dredged channel through tideland almost exposed at low water. Passing in its narrow confines one of the frequent tows of logs — massive rafts a house high and a city block long — can keep the helmsman's heart in his throat.

The tows are as frightening at sea as their highway counterparts are on the roads of the Pacific Northwest. The drivers of those logging trucks may have all the skill of Indianapolis racers, but their feet are mighty heavy on the throttle as they bully their towering rigs from forest to mill.

For the small boat, rafts create an additional hazard. Their huge logs not infrequently break loose. As they become waterlogged, the logs sink to just below the surface or even float straight up to spear their victims. Helmsmen must keep a close watch for this treacherous flotsam.

The channel, back in its banks going north, makes a sharp left turn and then a right, and there it begins to assume the character of a ride at Disney World. Off to port the trees suddenly open, and there, as if placed on a stage for our edification and amusement, is a typical pioneer western home. Against a wooded cliff that forms a lush green backdrop sits a tiny house of weathered boards, a trail of smoke weakly making its way out of the chimney. And not far away a barn, leaning against invisible supports, threatens to tumble down before our eyes, although paradoxically it gives the impression of having been that way for a long time. A small corral fits between it and the water's edge, where a canoe is tied to a rickety dock.

And now there, just past the bridge on the right, another stage —
a cannery to show us how fish are processed, packed, and shipped in
the modern era.

Then the stage for our main show: the waterfront main street of
La Conner. Like Port Townsend's, its two principal streets are layered
against the bluff with stairs climbing steeply to the top. Once a major
trading post, it too is now a commercial fishing center, but mostly a
tourist attraction with numerous bed-and-breakfasts (we used to call
them rooming houses), taverns, eating emporiums, and the inevitable
antiques shops. A long landing dock in front of the main street buildings invites the passing yachtsman to stay — if he dares to defy the swift
current to maneuver into a parking place between other boats.

Not much farther along, the channel ends and Anacortes is just
up there at the other side of tiny Padilla Bay, and right across narrow
Rosario Strait from Anacortes begin the San Juans.

Here, indeed, is the West Coast's answer to Maine — densely
wooded hills, soaring peaks, imposing rocks, secluded coves, pebbled
(and, very occasionally, sand) beaches, inland farms on the larger
islands, cabins galore, a couple of impressive resort complexes, and the
simple waterfront villages consisting mostly of a general store, filling
station, hamburger stand, and souvenir shop.

The differences that set this region apart from Maine are primarily
four: the greater abundance of fish and wildlife — after all, the white man
in significant numbers has been here only a third as long as he has been
in Maine; the superb ferry system that ties these islands together; the
mountains over which the sun must rise and set — Mount Hood to the
east and Mount Olympus to the west; and the comparatively tiny
package in which the San Juans come, geographically speaking.

Maine's attractions are spread along a 228-mile coast as the seagull flies, encompassing in its many bays and river inlets some 3,500 miles of coastline. By comparison, this mini-Maine is in a tight 20-by-20-mile area, but in that box are scores of island jewels, some so small that their colonies of seals and sea lions are the only inhabitants and others large enough to support the full infrastructure of modern civilization.

They are linked to one another and to the mainland by the squeaky-clean ships of the Washington State Ferries system, said to be one of the world's largest boat lines. The ferry is a way of life here (as indeed it is throughout the Puget Sound area). The ferries' passengers are an eclectic mix of camera-laden tourists crowding the open deck, commuters taking a noggin or two on the way to their weekend retreats, and bored lumberjacks and cannery workers staring out the windows.

When they aren't talking of the wildlife they've seen, the fish they've caught, the fire hazard (a terrible worry on these forested islands), or the threat of overdevelopment, they are likely to be talking of ferry schedules. Then conversation is impossible to follow by the uninitiated, but it sounds something like this: "I can catch the 5:12 to Anacortes, but it makes stops at Shaw and Friday Harbor, and if I wait and take the 5:25 direct to Friday, I might just make that earlier one back to Anacortes."

Orcas, San Juan islands

These huge white ferries, the largest of which carry 1,500 passengers and 160 cars, are a noble sight as they wind their way with sure-footed insouciance through the island passages. Although the hazards of fog and rocky shores are great, their safety record is remarkable, with only occasional aberrations, such as that caused by the skipper who let the ferry *Elwa* drift ashore one evening as he allegedly entertained a lady friend in the wheelhouse—whereupon a Friday Harbor bartender served the next day a new concoction: Elwa on the Rocks.

Perhaps the most interesting ferry stop is at Shaw Island, whose inhabitants include a number of artists and writers. Here four Franciscan nuns operate the little country store at the head of the ferry landing and are the sole tenders of the ferry docking.

As the ferry approaches, the nun on duty clutches her habit about her with one hand and, with the other, keeps her hood from catching the wind and bustles down to the landing. There she grinds the wheel to lower the landing apron and takes the heavy chain from the ship's crew to make the ferry fast to the dock. And then she collects the fares from the boarding passengers.

Neighboring Orcas Island was the residence of one of the islands' many distinctive characters. Henry Ellis retired as a successful engineer to a handsome home there. Always enamored of steam power, he built his own small railroad and engine to bring driftwood and supplies up from the beach to his house. And then he built a steam launch to go fetch the supplies from Friday Harbor.

Being a good Scot, however, he chafed at the waste of steam after he had finished his runs by rail or launch. So he built a steam calliope whose lusty pipes each evening sent "Amazing Grace" or "Bonnie Scotland" reverberating among the trees and along the rocks and rills of Wasp Passage.

In that and other narrow channels between the islands, the current can run swiftly, and our friend Tim Shepard, who grew up racing here, told of many a time in light winds when he grabbed a kelp root to hold his position in the fleet until the breeze came up again.

Life here in the San Juans is a twenty-four-hour-a-day appreciation of nature, its beauty and its bounty. The first-time visitor is apt to be astounded at both. You are as likely to get the fish you want for dinner from a line trailed off the transom of your boat as you are from the store, and as for Dungeness crabs . . . !

As we lie at anchor in Orcas Island's West Sound, nudging the cliff on its western shore and actually hearing the wind whispering through the trees overhead and rattling the peeling bark of the madrona trees, our skipper suggests that we might like a little crab to accompany the preprandial cockpit libation.

He pulls a tidy flat package in its commercial wrapping from under one of the bunks. It unfolds into a plastic crab pot. Taking the dinghy not fifty yards from the boat, he drops the baited trap and its accompanying orange buoy into the cold water. Twenty minutes later he returns to the trap and brings back four huge beauties.

The ocean's mammals are plentiful here, too. Pods of humpback and gray whales migrate down Canada's Georgia Strait and then through narrow Haro Strait, between the San Juan Islands and Victoria on Vancouver Island. Far more plentiful, however, are the orcas and the porpoises.

The orcas are known, of course, as "killer whales" because of a certain propensity for dining on other whales, but on the credit side they apparently do this only when extreme hunger dictates. These black beauties with their carnival white markings usually seem to be on an important mission, and while they'll let you come within a couple of hundred feet, they usually are too intent on whatever that mission is to stop and play. On the other hand, the porpoises squeak a greeting alongside and then play their game of chicken, swimming wonderful patterns back and forth across your bow.

I have a friend, Scott Lonsway, a charter-boat skipper, who adamantly maintains that Canadian porpoises are more friendly than the U.S. ones. "They come up closer and stick around longer," he says. "And they seem to enjoy the music more."

"Enjoy the music?" you are entitled to ask.

"Yes," he'll tell you. "We play the hi-fi for them, and they'll come around to listen. It must make happy vibrations through the hull. Most of them seem to like the sweeter music — the big band sound, Strauss waltzes, stuff like that. They don't care much for rock and roll."

Puget Sound and the San Juans and their adjoining waters are the last real cruising areas until San Francisco Bay. For the next 775 miles from Cape Flattery south, the coast and the ocean are not hospitable to pleasure-sailing craft.

The rocky shore and the sandbars have claimed thousands of boats, large and small. The few inlets of any size are guarded by treacherous shoals and most, like Grays Harbor, Tillamook Bay, and Willapa Bay, are too shallow over most of their broad reaches for sailing vessels.

Oyster-loving sailors might be reserved in their criticism of Willapa Bay, however. The Willapa oyster, rarely sold commercially outside the area, is a gastronomic treasure. No one who has indulged would question the neat little town of South Bend's claim to be the oyster capital of the world.

And incidentally, the marshes of the lower Willapa Bay, through which winds a small boat channel, have a lovely beauty of their own.

The majestic Columbia River is a case apart. The gorge it has carved for itself over its 1,214-mile rush from the Rocky Mountains to the sea is one of America's great scenic wonders. And along its shores western history was made.

Meriwether Lewis and William Clark, the first Americans to cross the continent, first sighted the Pacific from its banks on November 7, 1805, and knew they had accomplished the primary goal of their arduous expedition. Into his diary Clark wrote, "Ocean in view. Oh, the joy!"

Fur traders already had been dealing with the Indians along the river, and just six years after Lewis and Clark saw the Pacific, John Jacob Astor's ships of the Pacific Fur Company established the first permanent settlement in the Pacific Northwest on the south bank just inside the mouth of the Columbia. Their hillside fort and the wharf below they called Astoria.

The British North West Company bought it three years later and renamed it Fort George. Its original name was restored when the United States acquired the Oregon Territory in the 1846 treaty with England.

The Columbia is, indeed, historic and spectacular, and it is worth the ninety-mile push up its swift-flowing current to the bustling, lively city of Portland, seemingly so far inland that it always is a surprise to find oceangoing ships at its busy docks.

Where lumberjacks meet seamen it should not be surprising, however, to find one of the world's longest bars. Erickson's, with its 674-foot-long slab of mahogany, over which untold thousands of gallons of suds were spilled, was long a Portland feature, but unfortunately is now closed, although the building still stands.

To voyage up the Columbia, one must first run the tricky entrance to the river. From a distance offshore it appears wide and easy, but as one approaches and the bottom begins to shallow, the horror looms ahead.

When the tide is running in against the river's current running out, a maelstrom of turbulence results, compounded by the constantly shifting shoals over which the surf already is tumbling.

The secret, of course, is to run the entrance at slack water or at least in the hours when the current and tide are not in opposition. The Coast Guard operates a huge traffic light to advise boats when it is safe to cross the bar, but sometimes storms at sea, damaged equipment, empty gas tanks, or other emergencies, or perhaps a captain's ignorance of the danger or arrogance that he can beat the odds, cause boats and even big ships to try to run the gauntlet.

High above the water in the Cape Disappointment Lighthouse, a Coast Guardsman is always on duty, keeping an eye, by binoculars or radar, on the passing traffic, ready to summon aid when the occasion demands. The lookout might be a woman; the Coast Guard calls all its personnel, men and women, "Coast Guardsmen."

Help comes in the form of one of the Coast Guard's most valorous services. At the bottom of the road that winds down through the forest from the Cape Disappointment Light is the rescue station. When the alarm sounds, a trio of Coast Guardsmen wriggle into their orange flotation suits and strap themselves into their seats for the harrowing ride to follow.

Their boat is one of the most rugged small vessels ever built to go to sea. Forty-four feet long, it is made of steel and built something like a flask. It can roll completely over in the surf and come bobbing upright back to the surface.

Getting to a stricken boat and getting a towline aboard and getting its crew off are birds of a different feather, however. Sometimes the rescue crew wins, sometimes it loses; but when it loses it isn't for want of heroic trying.

Watching the scene below one bright fall day when the seas were running light and the fishing boats were working the now placid shoals,

I asked the watching Coast Guardsman if it is ever too rough for the rescue boats to go out. "It is the code of the service," he replied. "We are told we always must go out. We aren't told we always must get back."

The Washington–Oregon coast, so inhospitable to sailing, can be a delight ashore. There are cliffs on which the fir and spruce and pine almost hang out over the water and where one can picnic and watch the waves dance their ever-changing pattern on the rock spires offshore. And in contrast there are soft sand beaches, miles long and hundreds of yards wide, and behind them the honky-tonk strips of amusement arcades, fast-food restaurants, and motels.

On many of these beaches, stables accommodate the western penchant for horseback riding, and galloping through the surf is a popular sport. There also are rocky beaches where on fine days scores of visitors can be seen searching for agates, finely polished as the surf rolls them back and forth across the sand.

(And there are some portions so rugged that no roads even lead to them. Sixty miles of the Oregon shore, in fact, are so perfectly pristine that they have been set aside not only as a national preserve but as an international one under United Nations auspices.)

Northern California's coast, down nearly to San Francisco, replicates the Oregon–Washington shore—the wildness and the beauty from the land, the danger from the sea—and only one real harbor exists along the whole 325-mile stretch.

The entrance to Humboldt Bay is about as tricky as that into the Columbia River, and it too has claimed an armada of ships, including in 1917 the cruiser *Milwaukee*, which went aground trying to tow a previously beached submarine off the shoals.

Sixty-three years after the big ship's loss, an uncharacteristically remorseful sea decided to cooperate with a group of history buffs who had just voted to build a maritime museum. A storm suddenly created a sort of cofferdam of sand around the old hull and exposed it sufficiently for the new museum to acquire a small treasure of brass parts for its exhibits.

This is the Redwood Coast, three thousand square miles in which dwells the majestic giant sequoia, nature's tallest tree. It grows three hundred feet tall and sixteen feet around at its base, and some have graced this forest since before the birth of Christ.

They rise from the forest floor like the pillars of a great cathedral, and high above, as through stained-glass windows, a shower of sunbeams filters through their leafy canopy.

The redwoods also, of course, are a commercial resource highly valued for the strength and durability of the lumber into which they can be milled. The town of Eureka was founded in 1850 on the banks of Humboldt Bay to serve this new lumber industry, the first of a score of lumber towns that sprang up at the Pacific's edge in the next few years to supply the seemingly insatiable demand generated by the San Francisco gold-rush boom.

The lumber operators could not wait for roads or rails to be pushed through the wilderness, so they devised, with the cooperation of incredibly daring ship captains, a unique means of loading lumber from a harborless coast.

Towns were sited wherever there was even an indentation in the shore. Logs and lumber were sent from the bluffs above down to the ships by great chutes or, later, trolleys like ski lifts inspired by the same fellow, Andrew Hallidie, who invented San Francisco's cable cars. Skippers of the lumber schooners who called at these dangerous inlets named them dog-hole ports. "There ain't room in them for a dog to curl around" was the way they put it.

A little, highly maneuverable, two-masted schooner was developed for this specialized trade. Karl Kortum, the founder of San Francisco's Maritime Museum, estimated that three hundred of them were built between 1860 and 1884 before the steam schooners took over — more than one a month. Of course, attrition was high. On one stormy night in 1865 alone, ten were lost.

It took special men as well as special equipment to make the system work. As the onetime schooner skipper Fred Klebingat told Kortum years ago, "You couldn't use a deepwater skipper for that kind of work. He would die. He would die of fright. Sailing right up to the cliffs — you've got to get used to it. A deepwater man never did."

Few of the seventy-six loading sites remain, although the sharp-eyed sailor who dares venture in toward shore can still occasionally spot a twisted girder or dangling chain or other relic of a dramatic era in the West Coast's maritime history.

The dog-hole ports had names such as Rough and Ready, Iverson's Landing, Cuffey's Cove. Not much larger but almost luxuriously ample by dog-hole standards were Bodega Bay and Mendocino, the largest port between Eureka and San Francisco.

Mendocino, perched on a rocky, wind-battered cliff, was the center of all of this activity. In its lumbering heyday it boasted three thousand citizens, eight hotels, seventeen saloons, and twenty bordellos. Today it primarily is a tourist attraction. It has twelve hundred residents and probably more inns, boutiques, and cafés than it had saloons and bordellos combined.

Its settlers came mostly from the lumber towns of New England. Today Mendocino with its Gothic Victorian and Cape Cod saltbox houses is so "authentically" Yankee that Hollywood uses it as a New

England movie set. Angela Lansbury's long-running CBS serial, *Murder, She Wrote*, is just one example.

The *Orange County Register*'s travel writer, Laura Bly, said that there are many who feel that the Mendocino coast can't be fully appreciated without its foul weather of dense fogs and driving rains, and that is best experienced when you are "tucked beneath a lace comforter in a Victorian bed-and-breakfast with the smell of cinnamon coffee wafting up the back stairs."

In contrast to Yankee Mendocino, the well-protected little dog-hole of Bodega Bay is more like a Mediterranean village, with its population of Italian and Portuguese fishermen who still spread their nets along the docks for inspection and repair. The attractive little town, today inescapably also a tourist mecca, was the scene of a dandy environmental fight in the sixties over plans to put a nuclear plant there. The environmentalists won.

These places are not for the timid sailor, and they are certainly not overrun by cruising folk. Basically they are places of refuge for the fatigued, shorthanded passage makers when the frequent fog and storms offshore make running their nasty, rock-strewn inlets preferable to staying another night at sea.

Esther Burnham of San Diego, a veteran sailor of this coast, described the sentiment so familiar to deepwater sailors: "You run into those harbors at night or in the fog and you are so grateful to be inside, only to wake up in the morning and wonder what you are doing there. Fishing boats, broken-down docks, hardly room to turn around."

This is another area that it is better to visit from the highway than from the sea. Winding Highway One offers spectacular cliffside views as well as visits to the chain of Victorian logging towns.

And there are some special attractions like the "Skunk" train that climbs from Fort Bragg up seventeen thousand feet through the redwoods to the town of Willits. On its eighty-mile, three-and-a-half-hour run along a century-old logging path, it chugs through a couple of tunnels and crosses thirty-one bridges, some of them death-defying trestles. The original steam engine was replaced in 1925 by diesel, and loggers, objecting to the smell, gave it its present unlovely name.

Down the coast is the excellent reconstruction of Fort Ross, probably the most important historic site on the northern California coast. It was here that the Russians in 1812 built their southernmost settlement, and their most elaborate one, as they exploited the fur trade of the nineteenth century and dreamed of expanding their empire to the North American continent.

Fort Rossiya, as the Russian settlers called it, with 180 residents, two-thirds of them Aleut fur hunters and native Indians, was destined to last just twenty-nine years. Moscow's problems with Napoleon, a rapidly depleting stock of otters, and an increasingly testy Spanish government that claimed this land dictated the Russian withdrawal.

Mendocino, Lumber Schooner

A French traveler, appalled by the primitive, unsanitary condition of the Spanish missions he had visited to the south, exulted in the civilization of Fort Ross. There was a library and even a grand piano, although how it was wrestled up the cliff, history does not explain. There were formal gardens, a glass conservatory, and extensive orchards. Presiding over the little colony was the beautiful wife of Alexander Rotchev, the fort's manager. She was the princess Helena Gagarin, and one must wonder if she was an ancestor of Yuri Gagarin, the first man to orbit the earth.

Incidentally, the Russians at Fort Ross may have invented ready-built houses. The redwood pieces fit so snugly that they required no nails to be put together. The Fort Ross carpenters might have made a fortune even greater than that from furs if their timing had been better. Unfortunately, they were gone from America before the area's terrible need for housing was created by the gold rush.

John Sutter bought Fort Ross from the Russians a few years before gold was discovered at his mill in the Sierra foothills.

Rivaling Fort Ross as an historic site would be the place where Europeans first set foot on this northern coast—if anybody knew for sure where it was. Almost certainly the foot belonged to Sir Francis Drake, who back in 1579 had sailed his *Golden Hind* north after pillaging Spanish gold-shipping settlements in both Central and South America. But the intrepid sailor's log is unclear on the exact site. It could have been Bodega or Bolinas Bay or even inside San Francisco Bay. Majority opinion, however, places the spot on Point Reyes peninsula, that handsome outcropping twenty-five miles north of the Golden Gate.

Certainly it was on the beach here that in 1936 was found what some believe to be the brass plaque left by Drake to claim this land for Queen Elizabeth.

There is no evidence that Drake ever entered San Francisco Bay. He was there in June, a month when the entrance frequently is fogbound. If he missed it, he missed one of sailing's great sights, although it must be admitted that the addition of the Golden Gate Bridge nearly four hundred years after Drake is one of the rare examples of human's improving on nature.

That great bridge is a graceful proscenium arch framing the bay as one approaches from the sea. And then within that frame the picture begins to open until the wide expanse of the bay is revealed and, on its southern shore, there appears sprawled across the hills what the local columnist Herb Caen aptly named Baghdad on the Bay — glorious San Francisco.

Although old-timers complain that its post–World War II boom brought an alien culture of skyscrapers, high-rise apartments, and yuppie conservatism, their view is only comparative. The air of San Francisco still is giddy with the memory of its lusty, boisterous, rollicking, bawdy past.

It seems that the farther west Americans pushed from Plymouth Colony, the more they left behind their Puritan background, and by the time they poured into the little trading post of Yerba Buena, the bay's first settlement, there apparently was little left.

San Francisco's boating people are an exuberant lot, too, and they have a lot to be exuberant about. For the fishermen, as for those along the whole northern California coast, there are king salmon, steelhead trout, halibut, surfperch, and rockfish in abundance. There are sharks, too, prowling offshore and occasionally in the bay.

The great white shark has begun making more and more frequent appearances, particularly off Point Reyes, apparently lured to the coast to feed on the increasing number of seals, sea lions, and otters.

For the sailors there are 430 square miles of water on which to play in the bay itself, to say nothing of its expansive neighbors — San Pablo, Suisun, and other bays and rivers.

The fog that so often, particularly in the summer, hangs across the Golden Gate lifts much of the time just inside the bay, and here the strong offshore winds and heavy Pacific swell also abate.

The winds are still strong enough and the current runs swiftly enough, however, to provide some delightfully spirited sailing. It must be so, for a large portion of the bay's eighty-five thousand registered boats are sailboats.

Great cruising waters require destinations to cruise to, and the thousand miles of shoreline on the bay and adjoining waters provide them galore. There are scores of clubs, marinas, and waterfront restaurants to visit for a meal or an evening's entertainment, or coves at which to sit at anchor and enjoy the incomparable sight of the sun dropping into the Pacific beyond the Golden Gate and the lights coming up in the city.

At Alameda on the bay's eastern side and beyond the Oakland Bay Bridge, which gained notoriety in the 1989 earthquake, is the area's only sand beach, two and a half miles of it — although the view from there is sometimes obscured by an aircraft carrier at the nearby Alameda Naval Air Base.

South of Alameda, sailing as close to the mud flats as your keel will allow, you enter a bird-watcher's paradise. The Audubon people estimate that as many as sixty thousand birds have been seen flocking there — among them ducks, geese, cormorants, loons, grebes, stately herons, and the ubiquitous seagulls.

Although jets landing at San Francisco's International Airport roar overhead and Candlestick Park looms as a landmark on the

173

western shore, this spot seems remote from the San Francisco of raucous legend.

San Francisco has never quite lived down the debauchery of the Barbary Coast of its pioneer days, and one gathers that the San Franciscan is rare who would want it to. It is part of a culture that lives on the mystique of slightly naughty legends.

Those early settlers, fewer than a thousand of them, put up with, and many prospered on, a lot of carousing by the forty thousand rootless men and their camp-follower doxies who swarmed down on them in the first year of the gold rush. Five hundred establishments served liquor; no count exists on the number of opium dens.

But the good citizens rebelled at marauding gangs and wanton robbery and murder, and they formed bands of vigilantes to try to bring some order to the streets. Apparently they had some success. When the first court-ordered execution was carried out in 1852, it was reported that ten thousand spectators showed up — not to see a hanging but to see a *legal* hanging.

Stagecoach and train robberies were frequent, and on the lonely trails from the goldfields were found the bodies of not a few prospectors who never made it back to San Francisco with their pokes. The lawlessness extended offshore as well. Piracy flourished. Outbound ships with cargoes of gold were prime targets. One of the most successful pirates was a French buccaneer, Martin Thierry; as late as 1926, French detectives were still searching San Francisco bank vaults, unsuccessfully, for his loot.

Just across the bay from San Francisco lie lively Sausalito and Tiburon with their extensive marinas, picturesque houseboat communities, and incredibly beautiful nighttime views of Baghdad.

Also over on that shore, west of Sausalito and on the grassy cliffs of the Marin County side of the Golden Gate Bridge, there is a feature that the writer would be remiss in not mentioning.

Here is Fort Cronkhite, at one time a major coast artillery emplacement, named after a relative barely distant enough to spell his name differently — General Adelbert Cronkhite, a World War I hero.

(My distant relationship to California history has other facets, little noted, little remembered, and of little consequence. My grandfather named my father Walter Leland to express his admiration for the pioneer Leland Stanford; the Prussias, the great San Francisco mercantile family, were my grandmother's close kin; and President Franklin Pierce, of some relationship or other, was the one who gave Lieutenant Edward Fitzgerald Beale permission to bring camels to this continent to help conquer the Southwest. The president was not responsible for Beale's dedication, which prompted him to learn Syrian, the better to talk to his beasts, and to hitch them to wagons that he rode around the California countryside, driving a lot of drunks to sobriety.)

San Francisco had its whaling history, too. With a growing market for their products in California, many New England whalers moved their bases there and by 1885 operated large fleets in a thriving industry. It ended in 1938 with an international agreement to protect the gray whales, and the California Whaling Company called in its last

San Francisco Coast

vessels. Its old sperm-oil kilns are still to be seen on the hillside at Point San Pablo in the eastern bay.

The legends of the waterfront include tragedy and comedy. On a Friday in July 1886, the schooner *Parallel,* with a cargo of forty tons of dynamite, smashed into the rocks below the Cliff House. The explosion wrecked the building.

And to this day the little steam lumber schooner *Daisy* lives in San Francisco maritime lore. Lying at anchor off her wharf one day, she suddenly decided to sink. As her skipper conferred the next day on whether, or how, to raise her, she slowly rose to the surface. They never found out the reason for *Daisy's* quixotic behavior. She sailed valiantly on for years until she was burned to the waterline off Humboldt Bay.

Many of her sister ships met quieter ends, dying peacefully in their sleep, as it were. Their useful years ended, their owners simply ran them up on the shore and walked away. Some of their skeletons still can be spotted by a sharp-eyed sailor.

Part of the bay's allure is its never-ending procession of big vessels: cruise liners, freighters, tankers, tugs, and barges, and the ships of the U.S. Navy's Pacific Fleet. Some will dock at San Francisco's downtown wharves, but many will go on to one of the numerous ports that ring the bay or lie up the San Joaquin or Sacramento River.

Those two rivers, before they join east of the bay, define the delta that lies between them, an 1,100-square-mile land of sixty islands interlaced with 700 miles of navigable streams.

The islands are flat and featureless, many of them below water level and protected by dikes, but the land is rich in rice, asparagus, tomatoes, safflower, corn, and potatoes.

The delta is the weekend and vacation mecca of seemingly hundreds of boats, including a sizable fleet of rental, U-drive-it houseboats. White-trousered tycoons in their yachts share the mystic maze of waterways with apparently contented families fishing and swimming off *their* yachts.

Vacation homes and hunting lodges (ducks, they say, are plentiful) dot the islands, some quite elaborate. Hotelman Baron Hilton's Venice Isle Duck Club, for example, is a sprawling California-style ranch house with a distinguished membership and a guest list that includes some of Hollywood's more macho stars.

Tenley Island is owned by the Saint Francis Yacht Club, the bay's queen of clubs. Its "downtown" headquarters is a prominent feature of San Francisco's handsome waterfront drive.

On Tenley the club has built what its members call a camp but which might more properly be called a resort. Its limited sleeping quarters, for the few who might prefer to stay ashore rather than on their boats, are under a tent. But the grounds are beautifully landscaped, and there are two stages for entertainment, a large swimming pool, a mess area, and a definitely adequate bar. At one end of the island, an obsolete lighthouse that the club saved from destruction serves as an office.

In September this facility is the destination of the club's annual stag cruise, famous throughout yachting circles (and one of the most prized invitations). After a champagne breakfast at the San Francisco clubhouse, a hundred boats or so proceed more or less in line the sixty miles up the bay and through the delta to Tenley for three days of imported entertainment, good food, and a twenty-four-hour bar that keeps the general mood of hilarity at a fairly constant level.

Making the trip as the guest of the commodore isn't bad duty — particularly when the commodore in "my" cruise year of 1989 was Robert Ford, whose boat was the *Yankee*, a fifty-two-foot sloop designed by W. F. Stone and, as legend has it, launched unexpectedly and prematurely during the great earthquake in 1906.

The cruise on this classic yacht, this national treasure, was a voyage of contrasts. At Tenley there was a 120-mile-an-hour ride in Ocean Race Champion Howard Arneson's state-of-the-art speedboat. When it idled, its 1,325-horsepower gas turbine engine blasted into the air a missile-like column of flame, and its helmeted passenger indeed had the sensation that he was about to be sent into space.

As the boat skittered over the water's slight chop, Arneson's tutored hands played the bounces with the delicate touch that kept his baby from somersaulting madly out of control. The tule, cattail-like bushes, that line the bank were a blur as we flashed by. Then Arneson slowed down to a mere ninety or so, and there, in the comparatively narrow stream, probably less than a hundred yards across, he made a U-turn. His passenger was certain that his days were numbered in the seconds before the boat skidded into the dike ahead, but its twin hulls guided us around as if we were on rails.

Back at Tenley we entered a time warp as we stepped out of the next century into Conn Findlay's lovingly restored launch that Queen Elizabeth II had used for years to take royal parties to the Henley Regatta and other excursions on the Thames. Under its welcome canopy we took a leisurely three-knot cruise back along the canal where a moment ago we had been hurtling along forty times that fast.

Yankee's return trip to San Francisco took us near the tiny town of Locke, whose distinction is that it is the only U.S. settlement ever founded (1915) solely by and for the Chinese. Its three-block-long main street, with its two-story, false-fronted frame buildings, looks like one from a western cow town. Before World War II, its exotic gambling halls and restaurants brought visitors in droves, but most of Locke's young Chinese have left. Although some Caucasian artists have moved in, many of its buildings are falling apart. There are efforts to save it as a museum, but its future is in doubt.

That sail back — well, not quite a sail. The prevailing westerly that frequently provides a sail upriver dictates powering back. But nothing is lost to the first-time San Joaquin River voyager. As one leaves the agricultural delta, industry, big industry, appears on the riverbank — huge steel mills, sugar refineries, and the vast U.S. Navy Ammunition Depot, where a loading supply ship in 1945 blew up, wiping out the little company town and killing 305 persons. Pieces of the ship, blown hundreds of yards away, can still be spotted plunged like daggers into the mud.

Before the railroads pushed into the Middle West, San Francisco was a major grain port, and a forest of pilings of the long since abandoned grain docks grow from another spot along the river.

Marking our passage back home into the bay is the picturesque lighthouse on East Brothers Island, now a small hotel nestled into the rock. Accessible only by boat, it must be one of the coast's most distinctive retreats.

The last miles before we return to the yacht club take us past the San Francisco most familiar to tourists — formidable Alcatraz and the parkland Angel Island to starboard and to port Fisherman's Wharf, the converted chocolate factory of Ghirardelli Square, prototype of waterfront resurrection around the world, and the magnificent San Francisco Maritime Museum with its many restored vessels.

Leaving San Francisco is like saying good-bye to a sweetheart. One lingers as long as possible. The view westward through the Golden Gate is glorious, but the view back whence we came, this unique city on its hills, is still a view of Baghdad.

The bravado's coast of rocky shores, high and wooded cliffs, and distant peaks, with which we have become familiar since leaving Cape Flattery, continues south of San Francisco for another 250 miles to Point Conception. The hills are broken occasionally by brief stretches of beach and mighty sand dunes.

Back behind them, reaching up the valleys and into the mountain foothills, are mile upon mile of farms—hundreds and hundreds of acres of pistachios, pecans, pumpkins, asparagus, broccoli, artichokes, brussels sprouts, kiwi, and goodness knows what else. Gilroy, up there, bills itself as the garlic capital of the world.

That coastline is marked by a few features of some distinction. Monterey Bay is the first of them. This fifty-mile-long indentation cradles on its northern side Santa Cruz, so terribly battered by the 1989 earthquake, and on its south the communities of Monterey and Carmel.

Santa Cruz's popular oceanfront facilities—a half-mile-long pier of restaurants and souvenir shops, a boardwalk, and an extensive amusement park—survived the quake.

So did its yellow block-long 1907 casino, now an entertainment center, which is a landmark visible from far at sea. I asked a thirtyish lady tending a popcorn concession on the pier, a native of the city, what the building was called. She thought for a while and said, "You know, I've lived here all my life and I've always gone down there, but I don't think I've ever called it anything."

Monterey prides itself on being the first capital of what the Spanish called Alta California (Upper California), ignoring the fact that it was picked by error. The adventurer Sebastián Vizcaíno discovered the bay in 1602 and described it in such glowing terms that a century and a half later, when the Spanish authorities decided to colonize the region, they had their hearts set on it as their capital.

They sent Gaspar de Portolá north from Mexico to do the job, but Vizcaíno's report was so inaccurate that Portolá passed by the bay without even recognizing it. He found San Francisco Bay and was taken with its beauty and potential, but his bosses wanted Monterey, so Monterey it was.

It was no place for a port then — nor is it now. There may be no stretch of coast anywhere more scenic than this area, but a *natural* harbor it is not.

Where whalers and sardine boats once rode uncomfortably at long piers, an artificial harbor now stretches behind a long breakwater and is home to a large commercial fishing fleet and the boats of the Monterey Yacht Club.

Before the deteriorating environment, overfishing, and foreign competition depleted the catch, sardine packing was a major Monterey industry. John Steinbeck, native of nearby Salinas, brought fame to its Cannery Row.

The row still exists — as a few blocks of vast old canneries turned into stores and shopping malls and in one case, the most fitting use, the wonderful new Monterey Bay Aquarium. Exquisitely designed to show off some of the old brass cannery works, its centerpiece is a two-story-high glass tank in which a real kelp forest bends to the artificial current, and its natural denizens swim, crawl, and dive among the kelp's fronds — schools of sardine and the larger mackerel, rockfish, shellfish, white-plumed sea anemones, the incredibly ugly sheepshead — the panoply of a whole ecosystem.

And the hit of the forest, the murre. This little bird on its rock ledge at the top of the tank looks like a miniature penguin. It stands upright dressed in its own tuxedo — a white breast, black back and throat, and a little black cap on its head. The murre dives with amazing speed and actually flies through the water, propelling itself with its wings. It is so deceptive that many observers exclaim they are seeing a fish with wings. Incidentally, the murre here were saved from an oil spill. The aquarium is a rescue center as well as a museum.

Kelp forests are a major feature of the Pacific Coast ocean environment. They are to our West Coast what the marshes and tidelands are to our East and Gulf coasts, the spawning ground for so much of ocean life that they are the essential foundation of our entire food chain.

The kelp is rootless, its feathery base attaching itself with one of nature's miracle adhesives to a convenient rock. It grows at the astounding rate of seven to twelve inches a day. (Our aquarium guide, Gretchen Taylor, called the man who regularly trimmed the kelp their "haircutter.")

Its trunk is a heavy brown vine, four inches or so in diameter. When floating at the surface, it looks for all the world like a large plastic pipe. Coming on it unexpectedly can scare the devil out of a first-time sailor here, and it can, indeed, bend a prop or even entrap a small boat.

From the trunk sprout long arms of yard-wide fronds, the whole providing a habitat in which dozens of species play a perpetual game of hide-and-seek with their predators and their prey.

Arched Rock, California

The kelp beds provide exciting sport for the scuba divers, but they also are harvested as a commercial crop. Kelp is a source of iodine and is used as an emulsifier and suspending agent (in paints, ice cream, and beer, for instance). During World War I it was a vital raw material for the manufacture of fertilizer and gunpowder when the Germans cut off the Allies' potash supply. The bulbous growths in the kelp that help keep its sunlight-seeking fronds afloat were used by the Indians for bottles, and there are scientists today who think that in the oil-short future we may get methane fuel from kelp.

Monterey is the takeoff point for the deservedly famous Seventeen Mile Drive that winds through the pines and cypress of the Del Monte Forest past millionaires' mansions and seven — count 'em, seven! — luxurious golf courses.

One of the courses is called Spyglass Hill, but the craggy promontory upon which Robert Louis Stevenson modeled *Treasure Island*'s Spyglass Hill actually is Point Lobos, a few miles to the south.

The intrepid yachtsman willing to dare the numerous rocks and the mat of kelp can anchor right off the fabulous Pebble Beach course.

There are some spectacular vistas along the drive, such as that from Point Joe. Off that cliff is an ocean maelstrom of conflicting currents wild enough to put a timorous sailor ashore for life. Indeed, the turbulence has claimed many a ship.

At the end of the drive is the village of Carmel, which despite the pressures of tourism has managed to maintain some of the bohemian quality that brought its first fame.

A colony of freethinking writers and artists led by George Sterling, a prominent poet of the period, built cabins of various degrees of refinement beginning shortly after the turn of the century. The group included from time to time authors such as Upton Sinclair,

Sinclair Lewis, Jack London, Mary Austin, William Rose Benét, and Robinson Jeffers. The great muckraker Lincoln Steffens retired there to write his autobiography. The authors all wrote of the place, and Jeffers's poems particularly drew attention to its exceptional beauty.

So inevitability overcame Carmel, and after World War I it became a tourist mecca and a retreat for the wealthy. Escalating property values drove out many of the artists, and proper houses, although some of startlingly unique design, surrounded the remaining cabins.

Yet the quaintness of Carmel lives — its funky little streets sometimes dodge a particularly lovely tree, paths wander into the woods and down to the lovely beach over narrow footbridges, and the village, even in its "downtown" section of dozens of art galleries, a huge bookstore, and the usual boutiques, studiously avoids the horror (and convenience) of parking lots.

Carmel begins displaying its architectural diversity at the very edge of town. There stands a classic Spanish mission, Mission San Carlos Borromeo del Rio Carmelo, on one side of the street and, on the other side, a vine-covered, thatch-roofed Anne Hathaway English cottage.

The eighteenth-century Jesuit priest who pushed Spanish civilization into the Indian country of Alta California with his chain of missions, Father Junípero Serra, is buried in front of the Carmel Mission altar.

In the walled yard outside are a few surviving wooden crosses of those that marked the graves of 2,364 Christian Indians and 14 Spaniards interred there in the sixty-three years before the mission was abandoned in 1833. Many of the Indians died of the white man's diseases and the harshness of their treatment in his service.

Carmel also boasts, if that's the word, of a well-thought-of restaurant with the name of Hog's Breath Inn. (That, at least, is better than

Stalin's Breath, the first perfume the Soviet Union ever produced.)

Winding its tortuous but magical way south from Carmel is the forty-mile-long highway that engineers carved through the rocks, along the cliffs, and over the rivers of the Big Sur country. The highway's terrain is as rugged as Seventeen Mile Drive's is manicured.

There are some camps along the river gorges, some cabins in the hills, some extensive marijuana farms hidden under the trees, the memorial library dedicated to Henry Miller, who lived here, and the spectacular Nepenthe restaurant hanging precariously on the cliff — but otherwise this fog-shrouded forest is of unspoiled beauty.

Other than Big Sur, Lucia is the only town marked on the Big Sur highway map. It consists of a gas station on the side of which is nailed a sign that says it all:

1. Hearst Castle is thirty-eight miles away, one hour, yes, from here.
2. The bathrooms are at the right end of the building.
3. The weather is not always like this.
4. Civilization (as opposed to we who are uncivilized) is fifty miles in either direction.
5. Pay phones are in the next parking lot to the north.
6. Yes, you are in downtown Lucia, this is it, all of it.
7. Yes, I live here.

Also there is a sign advertising guided wilderness tours by llama.

Big Sur, of course, should be seen from the water as well as from the shore, preferably from a small boat whose course and speed for optimum sight-seeing one can command at will. This is still rugged sailing country, however, subject to sudden storms, heavy seas, and frequent fog. Sometimes all you can see is the bow of your boat, if you're lucky; at other times, only the mountain peaks looming above the fog.

But when you do get a view of shore, it is dramatic. The tallest mountain behind Big Sur rises to six thousand feet. Just north of Point Sur one grabs the binoculars in disbelief and then confirms that, yes, indeed, those are huge sand dunes perched on the cliffside perhaps a hundred feet above the beach.

The big round rock formation that is Point Sur itself is connected to the land by a low isthmus. With its lighthouse and naval station buildings, it reminded me from a distance of France's Mont-Saint-Michel.

Like all mountain areas, this shoreline changes color as the day wears on. The mountains hide the early sun, and their sides are cloaked in a mysterious blue shadow. At midday their colors fade in the brightness, but as the sun lowers, they begin to glow with a golden iridescence.

Toward sunset fiery spots appear in the hills — the sun's reflection in windows of cabins dug so deep into the cliffs that they are almost invisible from the road.

At night from a distance offshore, the flashing headlights on the cliff roads look like moving signs just beyond the range of legibility.

Sea Otters, Santa Barbara

Conspicuous from offshore are the bridges that soar over the ravines cutting through the cliffs. Just off one of them, Bixby Creek Bridge, a few miles south of Carmel, fishermen right before World War II made a discovery that, if it didn't please them, certainly thrilled the naturalists. The sea otter was back!

After fifty years of intensive hunting, the California otter was thought to be extinct by the mid-1800s, but here, a century later, it was back.

The otter, kin to the mink, rivals the dolphin as the most endearing of sea mammals, with its bright little eyes, tiny ears, and teddy-bear expression. It lies on its back and breaks open oysters, clams, and abalone by smashing them on a rock it holds on its chest — almost alone among the animals other than humans that use a tool.

Therein lies the problem with its reappearance. It feeds on the same delicacies that humans prize and that are an important element of the California fishing industry.

Today the battle still rages between conservationists and fishermen over the growing number of otters. A preserve has been created off the central California coast for them, and attempts are made to keep them within the park, but as their population grows, the otters are inclined to stray.

The fishermen complain that the otters are destroying their livelihood. Conservationists note, on the other hand, that the little beasts may be responsible for the recent rebirth of many giant kelp beds. They eat the sea urchins that destroy the kelp plants from which most of the fish come.

So the debate goes on, but to the passing boatman there are few shorefront sights as entertaining as the otter, lying atop a kelp bed, fluffing its fur, playfully jostling its neighbor, or happily opening a clam for a midday snack.

By the way, Partington Cove, where the otters made their reappearance, has another claim to fame. Legend has it that during the gold-rush days when the thirsty patrons of the Barbary Coast apparently would drink anything, a particularly loathsome brew was made out of the rocket plant, a kind of mustard. This so-called Rocket Whiskey was bottled a ways up Partington Gulch, lugged by burros down to the water, and then rowed out through the surf to waiting schooners. Some eyebolts remain in the rocks there to which the boats tied up.

South of Carmel the next really good anchorage is at San Simeon, a quiet little spot within a few hundred yards of the busy tourist entrance to the late William Randolph Hearst's opulent castle.

Not the outside pool or the inside pool or the statuary and artworks or the private zoo or the view over the 275,000 original acres of the Hearst ranch or even the fact that the lord of the manor maintained neighboring quarters for both his wife and his mistress — nothing impressed this plebeian as much as the Heinz catsup and French's mustard bottles he kept at all times at the center of his baronial banquet table. His mother liked it that way, it was said, but some psychologists have suggested that, amid the riches of which few ever dream, he sought to establish for himself the image of a western rancher.

A half-day's sail south of San Simeon is the comfortable little lagoon-like harbor of Morro Bay, distinguished essentially by Morro Rock, a 576-foot-high cone that sits like a beached whale at the edge of the shore. Locals think of it as the Gibraltar of the Pacific.

Unfortunately, the rock shares the skyline with three 450-foot stacks of a power plant that rise within its shadow. This doesn't seem to bother a burgeoning artist colony or the rare peregrine falcons that nest on the rock.

Another day's sail and we'll be at the Great Divide, at Point Conception, where the coast turns easterly and our weather turns fair. This marks the climatological division between northern and southern California.

Sailors call this the Cape Horn of the Pacific. The winds and currents can stir up a terrible sea off Conception.

The heavy fog that more than half the time shrouds the rocky coast compounds the terror. For the southbound sailor this stretch of ocean is purgatory before the heaven to be found around the Conception corner. For the northbound sailor hell frequently waits on the other side.

This was the scene of many shipwrecks and one of the U.S. Navy's worst peacetime tragedies. In 1923 nine destroyers, following their leader at night in a heavy fog, plowed into the rocks just north of Point Arguello, Conception's neighboring promontory. Only two of the destroyers ever got off the shore. Twenty-three lives were lost.

Driving down the coastal highway the change in terrain and weather is as dramatic as it is at sea. Behind Point Conception one drops from the mountains through Nojoqui Pass to the beach, out of the foggy mists into the sun as if emerging from a tunnel.

The landscape as seen from the sea from Conception on south to the Mexican border is pretty much the same — long beaches behind which are bluffs or gentle hills slowly rising to the various mountain ranges on the distant horizon.

Of course there are exceptional areas, such as the bluffs around Santa Barbara, or Malibu, where the hills rise steeply from the beach to form a dramatic backdrop for the movie colony's crowded and generally unimpressive (from a distance) beachfront homes, or the even more dramatic promontory of Palos Verdes on Los Angeles's eastern edge.

There is only one thing that the coast from Conception south has in common with the coast from Conception north: both have few natural harbors. As a matter of fact, the southern California coast has only one, San Diego.

Even the great port of Los Angeles, now the nation's second busiest, is artificial. Its location, based on the slight bay at San Pedro, was selected after a bitter fight between competing railroad titans.

The loser's nephew, Henry Edwards Huntington, in the end may have made almost as great a contribution to Los Angeles's future as did those who won the harbor battle. Huntington built the Pacific Electric transit system, which ran its beloved (and sometimes cursed) big red cars from San Fernando in the north to Newport in the south.

That streetcar (actually an interurban) system totaled a thousand miles and really accounted for the Los Angeles sprawl long before the automobile came upon the scene.

Los Angeles Harbor and its neighbor, Long Beach, lie behind the Palos Verdes peninsula, protected by an eight-mile-long series of break-waters. That promontory forms the southeast side of Santa Monica Bay, which begins twenty-five miles up northwest at Point Dume near Malibu, itself one hundred miles southeast of Conception.

The ocean south of Conception is about as benign for boating as it is anywhere in the world. The coast here runs mostly southeast and lies in the lee of the bad weather from the northwest.

Severe storms and the Santa Ana winds that come whistling through the passes from the desert occasionally require attention, but most of the time the winds are under twenty knots. For sailboats the problem is usually too little wind rather than too much. Frequent fogs, sometimes pea soupers, are the major hazard.

In 2000 there were more than 300,000 vessels registered in

southern California's five coastal counties, almost 95,000 of them pleasure craft. Sportfishing licenses numbered more than half a million. The boats were based in 122 marinas.

More than a thousand of those boats dock in the lovely harbor of Santa Barbara, a very posh city with expensive shops, expensive streets, expensive roads, expensive houses climbing into the forested Santa Ynez Mountains. The waterfront is beautiful. Cabrillo Boulevard is a wide promenade separated from the superbly maintained beach by a superbly maintained grassy, palm-studded park.

Santa Barbara probably ranks as the most attractive of the southern California oceanfront cities, but others are in the running, some for special reasons.

Newport Beach, for instance, is a boater's paradise. The onetime tidal lagoon at the edge of the vast Irvine ranch has been developed into a labyrinth of islands and waterways lined with handsome homes, yacht clubs, and the facilities to serve one of the most active and fun-loving waterfronts on the coast.

La Jolla, perched as it is on a spectacular bluff, is one of those picture-perfect California resort cities. Its architecture is determinedly Cal-Mex, and its atmosphere is genteel rich. Even its sodium street lights are subdued.

Collectively La Jolla's IQ must be on the high side. It is the site of the Scripps Institution of Oceanography, one of the world's pioneer and most prestigious such organizations, and the Jonas Salk Institute for Biological Studies, founded by the science hero who conquered polio. Nearby is the campus of the University of California at San Diego and the Scripps Clinic, both of growing fame.

Redondo Beach qualifies for special mention. It is about as lively as La Jolla is sedate. It has a famed pier of restaurants and amusements, even though today the pier is only half its former self. Once it extended over the water in a great horseshoe, but storms and fire have eaten away the center, and now it is two piers.

It also is the place where surfing was born as a popular sport. In 1907 entrepreneur Huntington, the streetcar man, brought George Freeth, a charming young royal Hawaiian whose father was a British army officer, to Redondo Beach to entertain at his beachfront hotel with his skillful surf riding. The rest, as they say, is history.

Redondo Beach is a major boating center. As is the case with the other such centers in southern California, an extensive breakwater provides its harbor.

In California's pioneer days along this flat coast, commercial ships unloaded or loaded their cargo by small boats through the surf. Later long piers were built to accommodate them. Storms have claimed most of these through the years, but some of the sturdier ones, now reinforced, are fishing and recreation piers today.

Over the last couple of decades, the state and local governments have built breakwaters at strategic locations and created a chain of marinas along the coast that now are the centers of extensive communities of hotels, condominium homes, restaurants, yacht clubs, and all the commercial appurtenances of an active waterfront.

They have given southern California yachtsmen varied destinations for a day's or overnight sail and are turning many of them from racing to cruising.

Noteworthy among them are the vast complexes at Ventura and Dana Point, on either side of Los Angeles, and the huge Marina del Rey with its six thousand slips in the middle of Los Angeles's Santa Monica Bay. Long Beach has its extensive and well-run Alamitos marina.

The urban waterfront and the extensive beaches are essential ingredients in the southern California lifestyle. California governments cater well to their citizens' needs. Beaches and scores of seafront parks are lovingly maintained. The citizens respond, and in almost every community there is at least one organization of volunteers helping to preserve and enhance the coastal areas.

At just the public beaches, where such things are estimated, attendance has totaled more than 75 million in recent years, and it seems to the casual observer that there must have been 75 million surfboards there as well. The lithe, tanned, sun-bleached blond look is all part of it, and a remarkable number of young Californians fit the cliché mold.

When the more daring surfers aren't challenging the ocean waves by walking the nose or shooting the tube, they might be found defying gravity in hang gliders. (Note: A few years ago a fellow named Cron built hang gliders he called Cronkites. End of note.)

A favorite cliff off which they like to jump is just outside La Jolla around the end of Torrey Canyon—the home of the Torrey pine, a rather scrawny tree whose only distinction is that it grows only there and offshore on Santa Rosa Island.

On the beaches and behind them are the glories that have made southern California world famous (and the mecca for just about enough people to destroy its greatest assets—open spaces and clean air). There are communities like Beverly Hills, Palos Verdes Estates, and San Diego County's Rancho Santa Fe, with their luxurious Spanish haciendas, redwood ranch houses, and fake pioneer farm homes shaded by eucalyptus, yucca, citrus, pepper, and ficus trees and surrounded by lush gardens of more kinds of flowers than a botanist could count.

There are the movie studios (Horace and Daeida Wilcox founded Hollywood in 1887 as a Christian utopia); Los Angeles's La Brea Tar

Pits, where they are still finding and exhibiting bones of the dinosaurs trapped there; and from the prehistoric to the modern, in Long Beach the largest airplane ever built, Howard Hughes's wooden Spruce Goose, so big that mechanics walked inside the wings to tend the engines. It flew only once, with Hughes at the controls, and then for just sixty seconds a few feet over Long Beach's Alamitos Bay.

Next door to the Goose at Long Beach lies the great ocean liner *Queen Mary*, permanently at rest in her bed of cement, now a city-run hotel, convention, and amusement center.

There is Disneyland itself and its neighboring amusement park, Knott's Berry Farm, and San Diego's internationally famous zoo, much of it done as a natural game park where animals range in the open, almost free.

The founder of Knott's Berry Farm, Walter Knott, was terrified when Walt Disney announced he was moving into his Anaheim neighborhood. But true to Disney's promise, there has been more than enough business for both, and the amusement park that began in 1920 as a roadside stand selling the Knott family's home produce now is extensive.

When Barry Goldwater was running for the Republican presidential nomination in 1964, the crowd of a rally he was to attend at Knott's was being warmed up by an actor named Ronald Reagan, of no political experience. As the candidate arrived and Reagan stepped from the platform to stand in the front row with the touring press, one reporter, observing the wildly enthusiastic crowd, said to another:

"This isn't Knott's Berry Farm; it's Barry's Nut Farm."

Reagan glared at them.

"That's not funny," he said.

There isn't much history to a country so new. Californians refer to the 1920s as olden times. Indeed, it has been barely a century and a half since settlement began in earnest.

But there are reminders of an earlier past in the twenty-one restored Spanish missions that dot the countryside.

Probably the best known is that mission just inland from Dana Point, San Juan Capistrano. Birds and astute publicists brought it fame. Swallows flocked to the mission so close to the same date each year that they were fodder for the tabloids of the time, stuck as the newspapers were with the peaceful doldrums of the 1920s.

The presumed phenomenon in which some saw religious significance has brought tens of thousands of tourists to the mission and created a souvenir market in the swallow theme for everything from fine Hummel china pieces to T-shirts and bumper stickers.

Unfortunately for the legend, the swallows aren't coming back in the numbers they once did. Insecticides used on the neighboring farms have gotten rid of the lure that really brought them there in the first place.

Of course, there is a downside to anything as glorious and popular as southern California—the smog, for one thing. To escape it, more people are driving longer distances to the suburbs, thus creating more smog. And, part and parcel of southern California's affluence, there are the oil wells. So much oil began gushing from the ground once it was discovered in Los Angeles in 1892 that the barrels to hold it were scarce and worth more than the oil itself.

Today the bird-like pumps still peck away in front and backyards and up and down the hillsides, and offshore between Santa Barbara and Long Beach some fifteen hundred wells pierce the rich oil sands. In Long Beach Harbor four huge oil platforms a few hundred feet from shore, in order to hide their naked ugliness, have been disguised as tropical islands with palm trees, waterfalls, and façades to make the structures look like condominums.

It seems to be nature's quixotic way that this rich oil field is in a highly sensitive ecological area. Santa Barbara Channel, as this twenty-five-mile-wide, eighty-five-mile-long passage is known, is on the gray whales' migratory track to their Baja California breeding grounds and forms the eastern boundary of the precious Channel Islands.

These eight islands lie eleven to forty miles offshore — the nearer, larger, and more popular all within an easy day's sail away from the densely populated coast across a usually tranquil sea.

Mountains, sheer cliffs, unexpected beaches, sweeping meadows, seaside caves (one of which you can sail into), wildlife ranging from native foxes to a rookery of the endangered brown pelican to elephant seals, trees and flowers that grow nowhere else in creation — the islands seem to have everything except people.

For their scores of unique species of flora and fauna, they are known as the American Galápagos. Five of them in 1980 became the Channel Islands National Park, and the waters around them are now a marine sanctuary. A sixth, Santa Catalina, is largely under the protection of a private conservancy, and the remaining two are military tracking facilities for the Pacific Missile Test Range.

Sailing to the islands at any time is a great experience, and thousands of weekend sailors do it regularly, but one is particularly blessed if one can be accompanied by a knowledgeable guide.

Jack Fitzgerald and Dwight Willey of the National Park Service took us to "their" islands, and we had the rare privilege of being escorted around Santa Catalina by Doug Propst and Terry Martin. Doug was the longtime president of the Santa Catalina Island Conservancy, which owns 88 percent of the island, and Terry was for years its naturalist.

If you are really lucky, the excitement begins on the short voyage across. In January and February you can sail almost alongside the gray whales migrating south through the Santa Barbara Channel to their breeding grounds in the lagoons of Baja California. (On their spring return north they seem to prefer a course on the other side of the islands.)

When whalers used their breeding lagoons as killing grounds before World War II, the grays were known as the "devils of the deep," fiercely attacking any boat, no matter its size. In a single generation they seem to have learned that humans through protective treaties have declared peace on them, and today they are positively docile.

Some years ago in San Ignacio Lagoon, we had one come alongside our rubber dinghy, gently nudge the boat, and lie on its side with one big baleful eye looking up at us. It seemed to enjoy being petted and having us pick barnacles off its head and sea lice from the lips of its great mouth, which was bigger than our boat.

About the time the gray whales appear in Santa Barbara Channel, so do the elephant seals. Ten thousand of them come south to stay until March, lying on the beaches of San Miguel Island. The bulls — the largest weigh three tons — establish their harems and fight to protect them; the females breed and calve.

Fitzgerald calls their migration a sight rivaled only by the thousands of buffalo that once stampeded across Yellowstone.

The elephant seal has made a remarkable recovery from the period at the end of the nineteenth century when its known population was down to a bare fifty. It had been hunted almost to extinction. Even its whiskers were valuable. They were used in China to clean opium pipes.

The northern fur seal also breeds on San Miguel, making nonstop the trip of twenty-five hundred miles from the Pribilof Islands off

Alaska, the only other spot where they are known to be.

At almost any time of the year, dolphins and seals swim off the Channel Islands. On our park service trip we altered course to investigate off our starboard bow a great roiling that seemed to stretch for more than a mile across the water.

It was porpoises. Fitzgerald and Willey thought there must have been two thousand of them, common dolphins for the most part. As we sailed in among them, some came over in friendly greeting and played briefly around the bow of our boat. Many of them seemed to be little families of three with a baby among them. In their midst a sea lion cavorted in an awkward imitation of his dolphin friends.

The track across to the islands is along the confluence of two currents, the cold California current sweeping south and a warmer current up from Mexico. They meet here and eddy westward.

On that current line squid, anchovy, and mackerel are present, and the line is clearly defined by the scores of seagulls, terns, and pelicans sweeping, turning, fluttering, diving over this sea-borne feast.

The islands, too, are affected by the currents, with northernmost San Miguel's waters twenty degrees cooler than those off Santa Cruz just a few miles south.

After Catalina, Santa Cruz and Anacapa are the most popular yachting destinations. The names of their small coves speak of the islands' history — for instance, Smugglers Cove and the caves under Anacapa's Vela Peak were used for at least a century by those beating import taxes or Prohibition. You can get a whaler or small skiff into the caves and up to the natural ledges where bootleggers used to pile their cases of liquor for transshipment ashore.

Then there is Prisoners' Harbor, where Mexican authorities unloaded the eighty convicts they put ashore in an unsuccessful penal experiment. The prisoners simply built rafts and skedaddled back to the mainland.

China Harbor honors, if that's the word, the Chinese fishermen imported to fish for abalone. The name of Potato Harbor needs no explanation for the visitor sailing past the round rock guarding its entrance. It looks exactly like an upended baked potato.

Pelican Cove is a favorite anchorage today, as it was in the twenties and thirties when people in the movie colony brought their yachts here. They left a souvenir for future generations. On the grassy hillside are descendants of some of the poppies they planted in an amateurish attempt to produce opium.

Frenchy's Cove is named for one Raymond LeDreau. He lived alone there for twenty-eight years, eking out a living by trading his fishing skills to visiting yachtsmen for a stake of grub and whiskey. He broke his arm in 1956 and had to go to the mainland for treatment. He was last seen boarding a bus bound north.

Some of the coves sport little beaches leading up into meadows that rise gently up the mountainside. Others are tucked dramatically under sheer cliffs that tower a hundred or more feet above them.

Scorpion Cove is one of the most picturesque, with its little island in the middle and a cave to one side — so picturesque, as a matter of fact, that it has been the stage for several movies, including the original *Peter Pan*.

Landing Cove, an almost perfect crescent beach, has a long wharf on which visitors gather to watch television monitors as divers with cameras take them on a tour of the sea life thirty feet below.

Landing Cove is just outside the zone off Anacapa Island that is closed to visitors to protect the biggest brown pelican rookery on the West Coast. The brown pelican in this area was almost written off in the

1960s, the victim of the world's biggest DDT plant, which poured its effluent into Santa Monica Bay. With the end of that poisonous production, the pelican has come back, and now some four to six thousand of them nest in a half-mile-wide natural amphitheater atop Anacapa's 936-foot-high Vela Peak. This peculiar bird, "whose beak can hold more than its belly can," gets quite gaudily decked out for courting. The pelican's white head sprouts a dark brown stripe down the back, its pouch turns blood red, and yellow feathers appear on the top of its head and on its chest.

My recorder captured this conversation with Jack Fitzgerald as we cruised off Anacapa. He was saying:

"In their new feathers, the males wait for the females to come in and then they select their partners. They bow and flay their heads around each other and they begin copulating, and they do that for a couple of days, and after . . ."

"Days?"

"Well, I mean off and on for a couple of days. And after about a week, they have some eggs to show for it. Then thirteen weeks later, their fledglings fly away, and they're all done with it."

"In contrast to human fledglings that seem to have a habit of coming back after twenty years or so."

Back in 1853 the not yet famous artist James Whistler was so taken with the islands' birds that he was fired from his menial job drawing charts for the government. His bureaucratic bosses did not appreciate the little sketches of pelicans and gulls with which he illuminated the corners of his work.

At least a hundred ships have wrecked on the rocks of the Channel Islands Park alone, including the gold-rush steamer *Winfield Scott*, whose bones can still be seen by divers off Anacapa. A Spanish galleon presumably loaded with gold and silver also is said to lie somewhere here, and the park service hopes for a future program to identify and locate at least thirty-five of the wrecks believed to be historic.

The greatest thrill on Santa Cruz is sailing into Painted Cave. If your mast is no taller than eighty feet, you can navigate its narrow entrance. Once you're inside, the cave opens up and the vaulted ceiling towers 125 feet above you. With many chambers leading off the main hall, the cave is so extensive that it even has been charted.

It is possible to moor six hundred or so feet from the entrance, where outcroppings provide convenient points to tie a line, and from there to take the dinghy for further exploration. As your boat glides carefully into the opening, you can see the pastel-hued rock that decorates the sides of the cave. From deep within, the barking of seals shatters the silence. An egret disturbed by your entrance gives you an acrobatic show as it flees deeper into the darkness.

Santa Cruz had half a dozen ranches from time to time and before Prohibition had extensive vineyards. But the most populous of the islands, and the most popular because of its proximity to the heavily populated Los Angeles–San Diego coast, is Santa Catalina.

It has the islands' only town, Avalon, of twenty-five hundred or so souls in the winter and twice that in summer. On its own little bay just thirty-five miles from Los Angeles and seventy-five from San Diego, it is a resort of remarkable neatness, including a crowded beach, the famed Avalon Ballroom, from which the big-band sound used to be broadcast across the nation, some spectacular homes, and the very exclusive Tuna Club.

So select is this band of fishermen that, in a dispute over the taking of illegal fish, they even threw out Zane Grey at the height of his fame as a macho writer of westerns. They only recently reinstated him, in a sense, by hanging a couple of pictures of him on their hallowed walls.

Their skilled fishermen take two-hundred-pound striped marlin, white sea bass, yellowtail, and, more occasionally now, tuna and albacore within a few miles of their clubhouse. That clubhouse is occupied by a noisy ghost who, as several members through the years have reported, occupies a corner room. As one club official told us, "We've never identified him, but we don't believe he's a member. He has never said anything."

Avalon has moorings for more than four hundred boats, some of them private; it is rumored that those for the larger yachts have changed hands for more than a quarter of a million dollars.

The many coves around the rest of the twenty-one-mile-long island are crowded with much less expensive moorings (but long waiting lists) for 749 other boats. Some of the anchorages are occupied exclusively by Santa Catalina stations of mainland yacht clubs or by other organizations, such as the YMCA or the Boy and Girl Scouts.

People from Los Angeles claim they sail to Catalina for its tranquillity, but when they get there, their boats lie so close together that they smell their neighbors' frying fish and are captive audiences for the neighbors' latest recordings.

Only one cove on the entire island is blessed with a solitary mooring. A friend of mine is fourth in line, should its present lessor ever vacate. He says he has contemplated serial murder to get it.

Outside the usually sandy coves the rock bottom and precipitous drop — a hundred yards offshore it can be four hundred feet deep — discourages anchoring. The only waterfront facility on the island other than Avalon is on what is called the Isthmus. Here the island narrows to a mere half-mile. On the channel side is a cove named Two Harbors, and a short sandy walk away on the Pacific side is a deep hurricane hole called Catalina, or Cat, Harbor.

These are the domain of the Bombard family. Two generations of genial Bombards have held the lease for the marina, the moorings (here and throughout the island except at Avalon), a restaurant, a small bed-and-breakfast in a picturesque old farmhouse, the island tour buses, the ferries to the mainland, and the shore boats that shuttle the mariners from cove to cove. The establishment's eighty employees utilize buildings left from a Union encampment of the Civil War.

This is the perfect spot from which to depart for a tour of the island with our escorts, Doug Propst and Terry Martin. They'll take us by jeep over the paved roads and on the side paths that climb the breathtaking hills and descend into the canyons and valleys that make up this rugged land.

They'll speak with justifiable pride of the job the Santa Catalina Conservancy has done to restore the island as nearly as possible to its original state by eliminating some of the predators, plants, and animals that humans have introduced.

Their most difficult problem has been the goats, brought here as a food source by the Spaniards two hundred years ago. They proliferated until, by the thousands, gaunt and hungry, they stripped the grass clean and left once green hills brown and dusty. They destroyed an unknown number of species of ground cover and the insects and animals that sheltered there.

Comfortably ensconced on Catalina are several hundred buffalo, some of them descendants of the island's original bison immigrants, brought to Catalina along with a lot of other extras to appear in a 1924 movie classic, *The Vanishing American.*

They are a picturesque addition to the scenery as they pose on the ridgetops silhouetted against the deep blue sky. Their wild state is partly conservancy ethic, partly practicality. As Propst says, "You can drive a buffalo anywhere — anywhere he wants to go."

With the sharp-eyed Martin to point them out, we encounter surprises at every turn of the road. There's a red-tailed hawk's nest with the female apparently feeding her young a small rodent, perhaps a squirrel. Here, in those yellow poppies, that lizard; it's a unique western skink with its shiny scales and bright blue tail.

We spot a Catalina quail with its cockade feather curling jauntily above its beak, a subspecies known only to the island. And there are ravens almost the size of chickens.

The prince of all Catalina's living things is the island fox found only here on the Channel Islands, and each island has its own subspecies.

The fox weighs about four pounds, two-thirds as much as its mainland cousins. But its outstanding difference is its lack of timidity. As Terry explains, "Hunted by people and surviving in an intensely competitive environment, the mainland fox is timid and wary and nearly nocturnal. The island fox, never having known man as a predator, is close to fearless. He inquisitively patrols the hills and beaches day and night. To a human accustomed to timid wildlife, an encounter with an island fox can be unnerving. This small mammal is likely to be as interested in its human visitors as they are in it."

As Terry talks, he holds on his lap an island fox. The fox is blind and was found wandering aimlessly on the single runway of the Catalina Island airport, a sort of aircraft-carrier flight deck perched at the top of one of the island's tallest peaks. It has a great view, but an approach that only a Navy fighter pilot could love.

Terry adopted him, and he became instantly as domesticated as any pet. As Terry holds him, the fox nibbles gently at my shirtsleeve.

The conservancy has been trying to reintroduce the bald eagle to the island, but so far without much luck, although we were treated one afternoon to a thrilling display by two of the present inhabitants swooping out to sea from their perch on the side of a cliff and diving to the ocean's surface with talons outstretched for the fish there.

The wildlife would seem to have an idyllic life on Catalina. Unhunted and protected, they live among yellow poppies, blue and white wild lilacs, white and lavender mariposa lilies, the white and black sage (which has a nice mint-like odor), the cactus, the honeysuckle, and the St. Catherine's lace, which can grow ten feet tall here.

And the trees are as glorious as the flowers: the stately ironwood, eucalyptus, elderberry, the huge Catalina cherry, the gnarled wild oak, and the Catalina manzanita, a large spreading evergreen shrub with dark red bark and green leaves and fragrant white flowers. (We won't go into the tobacco that somehow once grew on the island. The cattle became addicted to it, sickened, and died.)

All this once belonged to William Wrigley Jr., the chewing-gum man. He bought it in 1919 for three and a half million dollars. In 1975 his heirs gave most of it, forty-two thousand acres, to the conservancy. They kept their interest in Avalon and the ranch where Wrigley raised prize Arabian horses (the only problem being that the horses became seasick on the way to mainland shows).

Catalina's big occasions are New Year's and the Fourth of July, when hundreds of gaily decorated boats, jaunty sailboats, and two-hundred-foot gold-plated yachts with liveried crews pour into the place. The flotilla as they cross the channel looks like wartime England's heroic small-boat evacuation from Dunkirk.

Perhaps the only West Coast rival for such mass voyaging is the annual Newport-to-Ensenada sailboat race. With five to six hundred entries, this 125-mile downwind (usually) run to the Mexican port claims to be the world's largest such regatta. It almost certainly is the most fun.

Serious competitors use this spring annual as a seasonal tune-up, and there are some mighty racers in the fleet. But most of the entrants are what the *San Diego Log*, a boating paper, calls "fun-in-the-sun sailors." Whatever, they come from all over the West Coast to participate, lured by the gracious hospitality of the sponsoring Newport Bay yacht clubs at one end and the fun and games in Ensenada at the other.

The 1989 race was typical, except for the blue-ribbon boat and crew assembled to host this first-time Ensenada sailor. The sponsoring Newport Ocean Sailing Association under its president, Doug Wall, had put together 230 volunteers and twenty-three support boats for the effort. His Balboa Yacht Club hosted the pre-start captains' luncheon, emceed by the great 1970 America's Cup skipper Bill Ficker, who confessed to me he didn't like cruising. "To tell you the truth," he confided, "I never cared much for sailing. I simply liked the competition."

Starting 520 boats without a pileup that could only be rivaled on a foggy freeway is half the fun for the organizing committee. Off the Balboa pier there is much jockeying about in the hour before the start by the four thousand sailors on the competing boats.

There are crews in full pirate regalia. There is a crew in tuxedos, and another, an all-girl crew, in virtually nothing. There are jazz bands and string quartets and a bagpiper for good measure. There are crews representing the East Coast Ivy League schools in their annual race within a race.

This will be one of the slowest of the forty-two races so far. Hardly any wind the whole way down, but our superb crew keeps *Ms. Blu* moving, if barely. She's Harry and Jackie Thomasen's Swan 59, a beautiful sloop fitted with too many lovely creature comforts to be competitive in her class.

We have aboard a bunch of experts: the boat's regulars, Mark Christiansen and Bob Steel; Tom Ehman, a top sailor and America's Cup organizer; master artist and photographer James Gordon, who also happens to be Los Angeles Yacht Club's race chairman and director of the 1984 Olympic sailing trials; and a couple of second-generation Ensenada sailors with a lifetime of experience under their young belts — Linton Weiss, son of the race's general chairman, who at twenty-eight has seventeen Ensenada races to his credit, and Greg Wall, Doug's son, a veteran of three. In addition, John Busch, John Fradkin, Peter Huston, Greg Newman, and Clarence Yoshikane total well over a century of experience and thirty-six Ensenada races among them.

Our navigator and tactician is one of the great figures of West Coast sailing, Ray Wallace. He designed, built, and sailed from Europe Dana Point's *Pilgrim*, the replica of the vessel in which Richard Dana gained the experiences for his classic book, *Two Years before the Mast.* Ray also was the chief designer of most of the boats at the Disney parks and of the thematic waterfront restorations in cities around the world. He's a genius at it. He also once was Errol Flynn's skipper, but I have no record as to how good he was at that.

Even our cook, the ebullient, always cheerful master publicist Gerry Morton, is an accomplished sailor in his own right.

Actually as far as navigation goes, there isn't much to it. This is a straight shot with just one obstruction, and that provides the basic tactical decision of the race. The Mexican Los Coronados Islands, eighteen miles south of San Diego, sit astride the rhumb line, and the major question is whether to take them on the starboard or the port side.

The main island now is a Mexican naval station, but in the mid-1850s it was the headquarters of as mean a bunch of brigands as you'd ever want to see. They were mostly men who had failed to make it in the goldfields or even in the underworld of the Barbary Coast. They had turned to piracy, pillaging gold shipments out of San Francisco and robbing passenger ships on the way there.

The island was the scene of its own gold rush when good San Diegans answered the siren rumors and practically dug it up looking for buried treasure. It is believed they found none.

We drifted past Coronados in the dark on the inside, leaving it to starboard, and it must have been a good choice, for in the morning our competition was still out there on the horizon about where we had left it at dusk.

In lieu of more complicated strategy, some crews have been known to rise, or stoop, to rather inventive tactics. A Caltech crew scared its competitors way off course by broadcasting previously recorded sounds of a dangerously close shore: pounding waves, train whistles, trucks on the highway, church bells, crowing roosters, and barking dogs. And the captain of a boat drifting in a windless sea tricked his competitors into believing he had turned on his engine by using a charcoal cooking grill to fake a puff of smoke or two.

No matter what tricks he might have devised, 1989's light winds thwarted an attempt by Dennis Connor to set an Ensenada record with his controversial America's Cup catamaran.

But the game is to get to Ensenada, and the high times there and the ultimate award is not so much a silver cup as standing room at Hussong's, as deliberately dirty and lively a bar as a waterfront town is entitled to have.

The trip home is by way of San Diego and its post-Ensenada regatta.

San Diego, one of the nation's fastest-growing metropolises, stands right up there with San Francisco and Sydney, Australia, as a beautiful waterfront city. It has the huge advantage, shared only by San Francisco on the West Coast, of a natural harbor, along which its downtown has developed. San Diego Bay, one-half to two miles wide, stretches seventeen miles from its entrance under Point Loma, and its shores are dotted with marinas and yacht clubs.

The Navy's largest Pacific base is here, and majestic aircraft carriers, slinky submarines, battleships, cruisers, destroyers, hospital and supply ships, and speedy patrol craft are on constant parade past the city's mushrooming skyscrapers. They share San Diego Bay — sometimes begrudgingly, a small-boat sailor is inclined to think — with one of the world's largest tuna fleets, the usual commercial traffic of a busy port, sight-seeing and ferryboats, and a few thousand pleasure craft.

Inland fishermen will be surprised at the size of the deep-sea, long-duration tuna boats. These multimillion-dollar, state-of-the-art investments range up to 250 feet in length.

Across the bay from downtown on the Pacific beach is the historic old Hotel del Coronada, built for the carriage trade in 1888 and once the world's largest resort. Thomas Alva Edison was a consultant in its construction, when he could spare time from inventing the electric light and the phonograph. With its wonderful Victorian turrets, gingerbread trim, and broad verandas, "the Del" is as much a queen as ever.

San Diego Yacht Club, under whose banner Dennis Connor brought the America's Cup back from Australia but which was racked by controversy over the 1988 defense of it against New Zealand, is on Point Loma toward the bay's entrance.

Some of San Diego's water activity has spilled over into neighboring Mission Bay and its twenty-seven miles of shoreline, amusement parks, and the educational and interesting Sea World, with its trained orca whales and porpoises and its four hundred penguins in a replica of their natural Antarctic habitat.

The city so far has absorbed well the great immigration lured by its almost perfect climate, which is marred only by a trick weather pattern that sometimes blows Los Angeles's smog out to sea and then back into San Diego's face.

This is more than the old-timers can take. They are still jealous of Los Angeles's success in building a port where no port should be and thus slowing the development of San Diego with its God-given facility.

A few remember and are pleased to quote Maine's turn-of-the-century senator William P. Frye, who, surveying the tidal flats where the controversial Los Angeles port was to go, said, "If you Los Angeles people want a harbor, why not move the city down to San Diego? There is a good harbor there."

San Diego's waterfront promenade, the handsome Embarcadero, now augmented by a faux New England fishing village of shops and restaurants, is graced by three ships of the very active San Diego Maritime Museum. Under the direction of the world-famous naval architect Arthur DeFever, it beautifully restored the 1904 steam yacht *Medea*; the 1898 ferry *Berkeley*, which is full of exhibits and a working-model shop; and its prize, the iron-hulled *Star of India*, built in 1864 and today the world's oldest ship still under sail.

Every few years for a special occasion the museum recruits fifty-five volunteers to literally learn the ropes well enough to crew the ship on a sail out into the Pacific and back. There always are far more volunteers than positions, and the lucky ones — secretaries, brokers, executives, and laborers — spend a year of nights and Sundays to prepare for that one day's adventure, climbing to the yardarms, the nearest of which is 40 feet above the deck, to wrestle the heavy canvas sails or scrambling up the ratlines to the dizzying 128-foot height of the mast top.

The *Star* in 1989 sailed for the fourth time since her restoration with your author as the honorary sailing master. No duties but a load of fun.

Under the direction of its captain and veteran tall-ship skipper, Carl Bowman, we set sail with bands playing and crowds waving and a fleet of spectator boats as escort. Navy ships blasted a salute as we sailed out past history — past Ballast Point, where the Portuguese explorer Juan Rodríguez Cabrillo, sailing under the Spanish flag, made the first landing on this coast in 1542, only fifty years after Columbus discovered America.

We sailed just a little past Point Loma into the Pacific but far enough for *Star of India* to feel again the ocean's surge. As she lifted gracefully to its urging, I doubt that there was a heart aboard that didn't beat a message for her to sail on, on to where the west wind begins.